PHILOSOPHY IN AMERICA
AN AMS REPRINT SERIES

MIND AS BEHAVIOR

AND

Studies In Empirical Idealism

AMS PRESS
NEW YORK

Library of Congress Cataloging in Publication Data

Singer, Edgar Arthur, 1873-
　　Mind as behavior and Studies in empirical idealism.

　(Philosophy in America)
　Reprint of the 1924 ed. published by R. G. Adams,
Columbus, Ohio.
　　Includes Index.
　　1. Mind and body—Addresses, essays, lectures.
2. Behaviorism (Psychology)—Addresses, essays, lectures.
3. Life—Addresses, essays, lectures.　　4. Senses and
sensation—Addresses, essays, lectures.　　5. Science—
Philosophy—Addresses, essays, lectures.　　I. Singer,
Edgar Arthur, 1873-　　　Studies in empirical idealism.
1980.　　II. Title.　　III. Title: Studies in empirical
idealism.
B945.S653M56　　1980　　　128'.2　　　75-3386
ISBN 0-404-59382-8

Reprinted from the edition of 1924, Columbus. [Trim size and text area of the original have been slightly altered. Original trim size: 13.5×20.3 cm; text area: 8.9×15.5 cm].

MANUFACTURED
IN THE UNITED STATES OF AMERICA

MIND AS BEHAVIOR

AND

Studies In Empirical Idealism

BY

EDGAR ARTHUR SINGER, Jr., Ph.D.

PROFESSOR OF PHILOSOPHY
IN THE UNIVERSITY OF PENNSYLVANIA

COLUMBUS, OHIO
R. G. ADAMS & CO.
1924

PREFACE

We may not feel as confident as once we did that the way to truth lies all open before us the moment we have brought our vague questionings to a form that "leaves the rest to experiment." After the readings are all down, the facts all in, we have come to realize how much remains for the truth-seeker to do in which more observing will help him no more. But however we may have seasoned with an experienced caution the cheerful positivism of our fathers, in one article of their faith time seems only to have confirmed us. That blessed haven of rest, The Crucial Test, may no longer lie before us, our journey's end and an abiding-place; but never were we so ready as we have lately come to be, to give ourselves up for lost where we can make out no empirical sign to halt or help us. We know,—we think we know that questions leading to no thinkable experiment lead nowhere; having set out with no real object, they acquire no direction.

Is it an exaggeration, perhaps, and an impiety to suggest that our fathers—the most hard-headed empiricists among them—sometimes overlooked this caution of the way-wise?

Among the clearest and most engaging of the empiricist writings of the eighties was an Essay its author called "On the nature of things-in-themselves." No one would accuse W. K. Clifford of being a willing renegade to the gospel of empiricism. And yet when after the lapse of four maturing decades we recall certain passages of this Essay, how can we exonerate Clifford from backsliding? Can we even urge that his lapse from empirical grace was altogether unconscious?

PREFACE

Clifford had begun his Essay in the most approved fashion of the school by accepting "my feelings" as the data from which all learning-by-experience sets out. As experience develops, these feelings are found to arrange themselves in two orders: a "subjective" and an "objective." It is the latter physical science would establish by its observations, what then must it set itself to observe? Evidently there can be nothing *given,* whether to scientist or simpleton, but more and more of the same sort of feelings with which he started: nothing but these, though the object of his inquiry lie in the remote places of the universe. "If I hold that there is hydrogen in the sun, I mean that if I could get some in a bottle, and explode it with half its volume of oxygen, I should get that group of possible sensations we call 'water.' The inferences of physical science are all inferences of my real or possible feelings; inferences of something actually in my consciousness, not of anything outside it."

All of which is classic enough. And so indeed is Clifford's next step—only too classic; but with what impression does it leave us of the care classic empiricism took for the purity of its beliefs? A soul-trying situation confronts it. . . .

Assuming each of us to have been from the beginning immediately aware of his own feelings, a time must come when we begin to be curious as to our neighbors' feelings. These neighbors we have learned to know by observing combinations and sequences among our own feelings; but in this way we could know them for no more than bodies moving in our "objective" world. Now these bodies, so like our own, have they feelings of *their* own? How shall we know? If such other minds were objects we should know what to look for; for inferences of such objects "are all inferences of our real or possible feelings; inferences of something actually or potentially in our consciousness." But if classic empiricism is more

PREFACE

firmly convinced of one thing than of another, it is that *minds are never objects*. What then?

The moment is an anxious one. Will the classic empiricist hold the faith and refuse to believe in the existence of what can never be brought to the test of observation? Then his neighbors will have to go feelingless for aught he can do to save their feelings.

But just in time to preserve himself from this loneliness, the classic empiricist is able to bring his scientific conscience to admit an entirely new order of inference. How new, Clifford by no means hides from himself. Not that there is anything novel to the most objective science in the suggestion that it may take on faith the existence of all sorts of things eye hath not seen and ear hath not heard—*yet*. But in scientific inference, though "the existence of the [inferred] object .... carries with it a group of beliefs; these are always beliefs in the future sequences of certain of my feelings." (We may well call such beliefs "confirmable.")

"There are, however, some inferences which are profoundly different from those of physical science. When I come to the conclusion that *you* are conscious, and that there are objects in your consciousness similar to those in mine, I am not inferring any actual or possible feelings of my own, but *your* feelings, which are not, and never can become, objects in my consciousness. . . . However remote the inference of physical science, the thing inferred is always a part of me, a possible set of changes in my consciousness bound up in the objective order with other known changes. But the inferred existence of your feelings, of the objective groupings among them similar to those among my feelings, and of an objective order in many respects analogous to my own,—these inferred existences are in the very act of inference *thrown out* of my consciousness, recognized as outside of it, as *not* being a part of me. I propose, accordingly, to call

PREFACE

these inferred existences *ejects*. . . ." (Must we not call belief in such things "unconfirmable"?)

Is Clifford unaware that he is thus inviting every man-jack of an "empiricist" to entertain unconfirmable faiths? Beliefs in entities never to be "objects" of experimental observation,—entities that might well enough drop out of existence without the observer-of-his-own-feelings being any the wiser? Not in the least; Clifford faces the issue,—and laughs it off:

"How this inference is justified, how consciousness can testify to the existence of anything outside of itself, I do not pretend to say; I need not untie a knot which the world has cut for me long ago. It may very well be that I myself am the only existence, but it is simply ridiculous to suppose that anybody else is. The position of absolute idealism may, therefore, be left out of count, although each individual may be unable to justify his dissent from it."

The eight essays forming Part One of the present collection are a frank attempt to show that mind *is* an "observable object." The attempt must speak for itself. I hope it is not lacking in a clearness and definiteness sufficient to seal its own fate.

And yet, when these articles first appeared they enjoyed a unanimity of disapproval I can explain to myself only on the comforting assumption that I had made myself perfectly misunderstood. The thesis, "Mind is behavior," was new. So far as I know, it fell upon ears entirely unprepared for it by any previous suggestion that this might be the sense in which mind—whosesoever mind—was an object observable by all observers. The event might have been forecast: I was taken to identify mind with body. I was either an old-fashioned materialist or a new kind of madman.

Since then, the interpretation of mind known as Be-

PREFACE

haviorism has become famous enough. I have no reason to think that these unobtrusive writings of mine inspired a single pen of those that later took up the cause of "mind as behavior." It is more probable that the position in which empiricism was left by its "classics" had grown simultaneously intolerable to a number of restless souls. And even if it were otherwise, I should be in little hurry to claim the honor of having fathered or furthered the doctrine that now goes by the name of "behaviorism." Whether with their good will or ill, the writers who have added the "ism" to my simple reference to behavior, have managed to fetter the behaviorist with the "mechanist" interpretation of mind. I shall be disappointed if I have not succeeded in making it clear that all the categories of life and mind are to my understanding of them *teleological*. As such, I would defend with the best their right to a place in the most "objective" science; but should be firm with the most "spiritual" in denying to mind the meaning of mechanism.

To show the more living, the more spiritual objects of human interest and questioning to be such objects as can be approached by plain experimental methods is perhaps enough of an ambition. To have brought scattered studies so inspired into juxtaposition, that their import might be more readily grasped, their real faults separated out from their mere novelties of expression,— all this sufficiently explains the first Part of the present collection. But Part Two has a larger ambition; one that I fear me is neither so easy of presentation nor yet so sympathetic when revealed.

What does it matter after all whether life, mind, spirit be experimental objects, or mystical entities projected or "ejected" into the *Jenseits* of things-that-make-a-difference? Is our whole interest absorbed in saving the face of a certain philosophic school devoted to showing (but

PREFACE

having so far failed to show) how we "learn all things by experience"? Is the term of our idealism touched when we find ourselves arrived at last at a "radical empiricism"?

Indeed though, I cannot think it unimportant to practical life, whether we have or whether we lack a consistent theory of evidence. Men do not act on what they know for lies; but their driving opinions as to what is truth must depend on their conceptions of what is proof. More humane than soup-kitchens, more practical than cannon, must be every advance toward a sound theory of evidence. To rid any one such theory—empiricism, for example—of an outstanding inconsistency, is to have made such an advance.

But what if the very possibility of making this particular advance depends on a new conception of what "empiricism" means? If our attempt to be bitter-end experimenters has brought us to see the relation of experiment to truth in a new light, then, to mark all that is new in us, the adjective "radical" attached to our old sympathies will hardly suffice.

After we have patiently and painfully recast our old questioning formulas so that none of them—not even that vague groping for "mind"—shall longer elude all answer by experimental method, what remains to be done? More "radical" experimentalists we cannot become.

Our opening sentence hinted at our ultimate answer. We cannot with the heartiness of the classics leave all to experiment. Or put it this way: We must, more than ever, so conceive all issues that they can be put to experiment; but we can no longer conceive experiment to be that which puts an end to issues.

After the facts are all in, we said, the readings all down, there remains that for the truth-seeker to do in whose doing more observing will help him no more. Some

PREFACE

would call this more-to-be-done an interpreting of data. I should interpret this "interpretation" to be a moulding of the plastic material of observation, of the facts of experience, to the satisfaction of certain deep ideals. The exactest science is a poiesis, the experimenter with all his readings before him must turn "maker," our last image of nature is a work of the scientist's art.

I thought the second Part of this collection, through which runs this constant thought, might be called "Studies in Empirical Idealism." What obviously remains to be done in the way of giving to this thought clearer defininition and more systematic expression will not, I hope, have to wait a too distant occasion. Meanwhile, I could not forego an opportunity to attract the helpful criticism of my colleagues by offering my reflections so far as they had progressed in more convenient form than such a sorry one as the scattered pages of periodicals come to.

Permit me here to express my obligations to the editors whose courtesy has allowed me to republish articles originally appearing in the periodicals under their respective direction. To the editors, Professor W. A. Hammond of *The Philosophical Review*, Professor F. J. E. Woodbridge of the *Journal of Philosophy*, Mr. G. E. Moore of *Mind*, and Mr. John B. Clark of *The Mathematics Teacher*, I beg to tender my grateful acknowledgments.

TABLE OF CONTENTS

PART ONE
MIND AS BEHAVIOR

CHAPTER		PAGE
I.	Mind as an Observable Object	3
II.	Consciousness and Behavior: A Discussion	21
III.	On Mind as an Observable Object	33
IV.	The Pulse of Life	53
V.	On Sensibility	77
VI.	Discussion of Sensation-Intensity	101
VII.	On Pain and Dreams	109
VIII.	On Man and Fellow-Man	137

PART TWO
EMPIRICAL IDEALISM

IX.	Sensation and the Datum of Science	157
X.	Choice and Nature	187
XI.	On Mechanical Explanation	227
XII.	On Final Causes: An Abstract	261
XIII.	Kant's First Antinomy: The Question of Fact	267
XIV.	The Mathematician and His Luck	285

PART ONE

MIND AS BEHAVIOR

MIND AS AN OBSERVABLE OBJECT

I.

MIND AS AN OBSERVABLE OBJECT [1]

It is seldom given to philosophers to enter into one another's enthusiasms, but they are sometimes allowed to share a disappointment. And could anything be more generally disappointing than the attitude of a certain important group of natural philosophers toward the study of minds? I refer to that curious bit of reasoning commonly known as the "analogy argument" which runs somehow thus: I am aware, and I alone am aware, that certain of my bodily acts are accompanied by mental states. When I observe similar acts in other bodies I infer that they too are accompanied by like states of mind. No experience can be brought to confirm this inference, but then nothing can transpire to refute it. Meanwhile, my feelings are spared a severe strain by risking it—the loneliness of not risking it is too tragic to be faced.

The objectionable points of this line of argument are just all the points of its make-up. To begin with, it is so far from self-evident that each

[1] Paper read before the American Philosophical Association at Princeton, December, 1910.

man's mental state is his own indisputable possession, no one hesitates to confess at times that his neighbor has read him better than he has read himself, nor at other times to claim that he knows his neighbor's state of mind more truly than the neighbor himself knows it. No one finds fault with Thackeray for intimating that the old Major is a better judge of Pendennis's feeling for the Fotheringay than is Pendennis himself. To be sure, we are more likely to accept such situations when the state of mind read from the outside is complex and subtle; but there should be no difference in principle between the diagnosis of love and a test for color-blindness. It is quite as likely that under certain conditions I do not know what red is, as that under other conditions I do not know what love is. In a word, so long as we are social beings our judgments, even the simplest of them, have social meanings, and each knows himself through others.

Next, the analogy argument calls its procedure an inference. Now, everybody knows an inference from a thousand cases to be more valuable than one drawn from a hundred, an anticipation based on a hundred observations to be safer than one with only ten to support it. But there are those who, knowing all this, would conclude that an inference from one instance has *some* value.

MIND AS AN OBSERVABLE OBJECT

If in my case mental states accompany my body's behavior, there is at least *some* ground for supposing like acts of another's body to be in like manner paralleled. This illusion, for it is one, springs I think from a failure to catch the meaning of inference. An inference from a single case, if it be really an inference from a single case, has exactly no value at all. No one would be tempted to attribute eight planets to every sun because our sun has eight such satellites. The reason a single observation is sometimes correctly assumed to have weight is that the method of observing has been previously tested in a variety of cases. The shop-keeper measures his bit of fabric but once; he has however measured other fabrics by the same method numberless times, and has a fairly clear idea of the probable error of his result. But the principle holds absolutely of all results: no series of observations, no probable error; no ground for inference; no meaning as a datum.

Nor is our line of argument happier in its next point. The hypothesis of other minds is one that must be regarded as referring to the *Jenseits* of things that make a difference to my experience. There is a fair definition of pragmatism to be found among the last sayings of the man whose absence this day leaves us lonely indeed; a definition tempting me to think I have always been, in all innocence, a pragmatist:

"The serious meaning of a concept," writes James, following Peirce, "lies in the concrete difference to some one which its being true will make. Strive to bring all debated conceptions to that "pragmatic" test, and you will escape vain wrangling. . . . If it can make no practical difference whether a given statement be true or false, then the statement has no real meaning." [1]

If the method defined in this passage be accepted, and I can not see how any one can fail to accept it even if one prove unfaithful to it afterwards, then could anything more fully illustrate the meaning of the 'meaningless' than that hypothesis of other minds in which the analogy argument culminates? Whatever may be said for the reasoning, is its conclusion at least right? Alas, I can not know. If right, my experience cannot inform me; if wrong, my experience cannot disillusion me. It makes no practical difference to me whether I am right or wrong. Pragmatic conclusion: I cannot have made a meaningful hypothesis.

But here I hesitate. The same writer whose definition of method I was eager to accept as pointing the lack of meaning in the hypothesis under consideration, is capable of interpreting his own

[1] "Meaning of Truth," p. 52.

MIND AS AN OBSERVABLE OBJECT

words, "that which makes a practical difference," in a way one might be excused for having overlooked as a possibility. He had once said—quite as we should have expected him to say—that " 'God' and 'matter' might be regarded as synonymous terms so long as no differing future consequences were deducible from the two conceptions." Should we not equally have expected him to say that a soulful neighbor and a soulless one were synonymous terms so long as the two neighbors treated us in the same way? Yet not only does he refuse to go so far, but, coming face to face with the problem, he hastily retraces steps already ventured. "I had no sooner given the address [containing the statement respecting 'God' and 'matter'] than I perceived a flaw in that part of it. . . . The flaw was evident when, as a case analogous to that of a godless universe, I thought of what I called an 'automatic sweetheart,' meaning a soulless body, which should be absolutely indistinguishable from a spiritually animated maiden, laughing, talking, blushing, nursing us, and performing all feminine offices as tactfully and as sweetly as if a soul were in her. Would any one regard her as a full equivalent? Certainly not, and why? Because, framed as we are, our egoism craves above all things inward sympathy and recognition, love and admiration. The outward treatment is valued mainly as an expression, as a manifestation of the accompanying consciousness believed in. Pragmatically, then, belief in an automatic sweetheart would not *work*, and in point of fact no one treats it as a serious hypothesis. The godless universe would be exactly similar. Even if matter could do every outward thing that God does, the idea of it would not *work* as satisfactorily, because the chief call for a God on modern men's part is for a being who will inwardly recognize them and judge them sympathetically. Matter disappoints this craving of our ego; so God remains for most men the truer hypothesis, and indeed remains so for definite pragmatic reasons." [1]

I conceive that no criticism could make heavier the burden of disappointment these words of their own weight carry with them into the soul of any man who, having found no better *reason* for believing in God and his fellows than the analogy argument furnishes, now finds no better *motive* for believing than this kind of pragmatism holds forth. Instead of criticizing, let me use the picture to contrast with it another which, in spite of certain elements that may at first sight offend previous ideas on the subject of soul, must at least satisfy the reason of an empiricist.

No, I suppose no one would regard a soulless

[1] "Meaning of Truth," p. 189 sqq., note.

sweetheart as a full equivalent for a soulful one, as these words "soulless" and "soulful" are ordinarily used. But just there is the point: how are they ordinarily used? If I imagine myself come to believe that my mistress, with all her loveliness, is really without soul, I cannot think what I should mean by this if it be not that I fear her future conduct will not bear out my expectations regarding her. Some trait or gesture, a mere tightening of the lips, hardening of the eye, stifling of a yawn, one of those things we say are rather felt than seen, would have raised in my mind the suspicion that she might not to my fuller experience of her remain indistinguishable from a spiritually minded maiden. Aye, now I come to think of it, has she ever been except to my blinded eyes indistinguishable from one who had that "inward sympathy and recognition, love and admiration, which above all things my egoism craves"?

Isn't this what we mean by the practical issue involved in the disjunction—soul or no soul? Of course they are not equivalent, these two, and they are not so just because a soul is not the kind of thing the analogy argument takes it to be. It would never occur to me to try to hold this suspicioned lady's soul by tying an eject around her neck. What she is for me and what she is *an sich* constitutes just such a difference, now that it is a question of a soul, as it would were any other fact of nature up for discussion. The poorer and the fuller experience of the thing, these and these alone define such a difference.[1] I am afraid to know my sweetheart better lest I come upon that trait of her behavior which would only too surely distinguish her from the soul-inspired maiden I had taken her to be. If, *per impossibile*, I could be assured that no such trait of behavior would ever reveal itself to the fullest experience, and if the hypothesis were still thrust upon me that she might nevertheless be without soul, my feelings would react as they might be expected to were one to assure me that a given figure must prove to all possible observation three-sided and plane enough, yet might *an sich* be without triangularity.

If my analysis of this concrete situation has not been too badly received, I shall have courage to utter the full thought that lies behind all these criticisms and suggestions. It is this:

Consciousness is not something inferred from behavior; it *is* behavior. Or, more accurately: Our belief in consciousness is an expectation of probable behavior based on an observation of actual behavior, a belief to be confirmed or refuted by

[1] *Cf.*, pp. 279-282.

more observation as any other belief in a fact is to be tried out.

You will ask me: What aspect of the behavior of certain objects leads us to call them conscious? I answer, I do not know, and expect never surely to know. Had I been asked: What aspect of the behavior of certain objects leads us to call them alive? I must have returned the same answer. The deep blind instincts of the race, slowly working themselves out into the classifications we now so readily accept and so facilely apply, these instincts are not easily to be enticed out into the light of day. But though I don't know what *life* means, nor what *consciousness* means, I feel that I know how we may go to work to find out these things, if once we see that neither stands for an eject forever veiled and hidden in the land beyond experience. Instead, then, of venturing a word where a long and patient analysis would alone suffice, I may confine myself to the weighing of certain objections that would attack the very method here suggested for finding out what consciousness means.[1]

The whole situation out of which the analogy argument springs is that seized upon by English "sensualism." Here the essential idea is that I have certain immediate data, recognizable and namable

[1] An analysis of the concepts *life* and *mind* will now be found in Articles IV-VII of this collection.

each by itself. Out of these simple ideas (whether of sensation alone or of sensation and reflection) I build my world of objects, including my own body and the bodies of other humans. If I am to suppose these other beings have minds at all, I must suppose their minds to work in the same way to build up a world in which my body is an object. But if they do, then they start from data as independent of any reference to mine as I assume mine to have been of any allusion to theirs.

To one who cannot rid himself of this way of philosophizing, it is impossible that any analysis of behavior I might undertake should prove satisfying. The whole idea of my thesis would be simply an absurdity. For—and if I have not emphasized the point sufficiently I now take the opportunity to do so—it is essential to my thesis that I regard my own mind as behavior, quite as frankly as I take my fellow's mind to be nothing else. It is of course a *type* of behavior that is in question, and it is my observation that I act like or unlike others in certain situations which makes me class my experience as of such and such a kind. If the part of my behavior dependent on my eyes being open and directed toward an object is identical when that object is blood and when it is grass, while that of other men similarly placed is different toward the two, I judge myself to have only one color-sensation where they have two. In all such cases my notion of my mental state, as also the fact that I have any notion on the subject at all, is dependent upon my observation of behavior. It is impossible that any one should come even a first step toward agreeing with me if he is wedded to the theory of experience that starts with a datum as a mason starts with a brick or a chemist with an atom.

I have on a former occasion before this association accepted the thesis that there is no such datum, and as even at that time there seemed to me nothing novel in such acceptance, but merely an insistence that we should not keep on forgetting what we had sometime accepted as true, I need not argue the point here.[1] As nearly as so complex a matter can be put in a few words, the thought is this: The beginning of our epistemological building is not a datum which might be known by itself, not, *e. g.*, the first sensation of a babe *in utero* or of a Condillac statue, but just any point at which it occurs to us to ask ourselves, What is it you know? and, How do you know it? From this point—it may as well be for a Newton the evening of the day he has given to the world his law of gravitation—from this point stretch out two wearily endless ways. The one leads toward, but

[1] *Vid.* p. 157 sqq., ''Sensation and the Datum of Science.''

never arrives at, the real object; the other leads toward, but never culminates in, the bare datum. We shall never have the one before the other, nor yet come nearer to the one save as we come nearer the other. Sensualism is the philosophy of the impatient thinker who will arrive at all costs—the analogy argument is one of the costs.

But when I have made sensualistic philosophy the soil from which the analogy argument favorably springs, I have not yet dug down to the roots. The whole attitude toward souls and the relation of souls to bodies which makes the outcome of "analogy" seem meaningful, even if regrettably insecure, is the result of habits of thought much older than those guiding the highly reflective procedure of a Locke or of a Hume. These primitive habits are intimately mixed with ethical motives, yet I think their deepest significance is to be caught by viewing them as early attempts at scientific method.

From this point of view, one must realize what satisfaction the most unreflective mind has in treating any complex thing as an additive result, a sum of simpler things. This instinct for adding might be illustrated almost indefinitely; but one or two instances will serve to show how addition has been used and abused.

MIND AS AN OBSERVABLE OBJECT

We are barely through those long chapters in the history of science in which the theory of a hot body composed that object of a body plus heat. This heat was first conceived as itself a kind of body—a congeries of small round atoms; then, since heat did not increase the mass to which it was added, it became the vaguer stuff called "caloric." Nevertheless, however ghostly this caloric had become, it still went in and out of bodies like a stuff; fell under the same principle of individuation that bodies fall under; was in short a sort of body, though a mysterious sort of body. We know with what travail this strong, primitive instinct to add was overcome, and men had the courage to say, "Heat is not something inferred from the heated behavior of a body; it *is* that behavior. A hot body differs from a cold body only in the way its parts move." The mystery had vanished. A quantity of heat had no longer an individuality of its own, but if it could be said to travel, it did so as a wave travels, and the theory of its nature became clear.

Again, we see this same instinct to add in a theory of life not yet past, perhaps, but certainly passing. As a hot body is a body plus heat, so a living body is a carcass plus life. The history of this conception is strikingly like that of the previous one. At first the thing added to body to make it alive was another body—the "psyche"—differing, may be, in certain of its qualities, but still falling under the same principles of individuation, having a history of its own when disembodied. Now, this psyche is reduced where it survives at all to that vague principle called "the vital," of which all that can be said is that it is a mystery. Few thinkers cling to this survival; for most of us a living body is a mechanism that behaves in a certain way, in a way well-calculated to attain certain ends. Life is no longer a thing to be inferred from behavior; it *is* behavior, and while it is an aspect of a body's behavior from which other aspects may be distinguished, we no longer think of these aspects as separable. Disembodied life has been placed among the myths.

And now, should we not expect the same instinct-to-add to have played a part in our theory of consciousness? Aristotle, close as was his doctrine of "forms" to the treatment of life advocated in this paper, yet fell into the old habit when he composed a rational animal of an animal plus a rational soul "come from without." Descartes, close as he was to the theory that a living body is a mechanism behaving in a certain purposeful way, had yet to compose a human being of such a living body and a soul perched in the pineal gland. Are we so far from this when we confection a real sweetheart of an automatic one and an eject? To be sure the eject is not located and the kind of individuality it may have is not specified; but therewith we have taken from the added-on soul the last thinkable trait it possessed. It has now the complete mystery of the meaningless.

Have we not come to the point of realizing the meaninglessness of the mystery?

CONSCIOUSNESS AND BEHAVIOR:
A DISCUSSION

II.

CONSCIOUSNESS AND BEHAVIOR: A DISCUSSION

"What shall deliver the deliverer?"

Professor Miller asks the question at the end of a "discussion" [1] of my paper on "Mind as an Observable Object." It is I who am the "deliverer," but of what a sorry sort will be gathered from the answer Mr. Miller finds to his own question.

> What shall deliver the deliverer himself? Nothing but a taste for real solutions—which is the same as intellectual scruple. Nothing but common sense untired—which is the same as pertinacity in logic. Nothing but looking about us before we advance—sweeping the horizon of our subject—circumspection; that last rule of Descartes's method, followed as far as human vision can, ''to make enumerations so complete and reviews so general that I might be assured that nothing was omitted.''

One would like to have contributed something better than the inspiration of a bad example to sentiments so just.

But Mr. Miller is no unkindly critic. He is good enough to say that some earlier work of mine promised better things—that even now I may have better things in reserve. Perhaps, too, it occurred to Mr. Miller that a twenty-minute paper

[1] *Journal of Philosophy*: VIII, pp. 322-327.

left me little room for enumerations so complete and reviews so general that I might be assured nothing was omitted. Something in the way of enumeration and review that I had tried before writing quite brought it home to me that sacrifices were demanded. I thought I might begin by passing over the *ungereimte Frage*.

However happy this idea, I know it would have been happier if men stood in closer agreement as to what *meaning* meant. But then the history of philosophy would be the shortest of stories, the love of wisdom would not long go unrequited, thought would lie listless in the pervading calm —and I should have missed a critic of flavor. It did seem to me, though, that some questions were beyond question—as, for example, What shall we call that which can have no name?

I know that many with "a taste for real solutions" have answered, An immediate fact of consciousness. Out of such facts taken together they make a "field," and out of such fields a world. But what in the world is consciousness? Across these fields, dust of their dust, passes the occasional figure of a fellow-being. For his brother-likeness to the owner of the field, this passing figure is given a field of his own—one from which the giver is forever excluded. Straightway the donor grows anxious for his gift. Does the one to whom it has been given really have the thing just given to him? Then where in the world is *his* consciousness?

No one can blame the dwellers in such a world if they cry aloud for deliverance, least of all one who remembers to have lived there and to have been unhappy there—one who might still be unhappily living there had he waited with the others for a deliverer who could work miracles.

Very pleasantly Mr. Miller quotes *à mon intention* the saying of a certain Old Lady: "We must all make a little effort every day to keep sane and use words in the same senses." Which, being applied, I take to mean that the deliverer Mr. Miller awaits must begin by accepting "consciousness" in the sense those who would be delivered have given to the word. He must make a little effort every day to keep on using the term in this same sense. He must start at the same point and travel the same road, but he shall reach the goal of intelligibility at last without having been downed by any of those contradictions that have been the undoing of all who have so started and so traveled. Then, and only then, shall we know him for the true deliverer by the miracle he has wrought.

Meanwhile, for one who is too impatient to await the impossible, there lies close to hand a suggestion so natural it can excite no enthusiasm, so simple it may inspire mockery, and so little in the "same sense" with what has gone before that the Old Lady of Good Counsel would not have it to be sane. It is this: Let us make our way out of a troubled world by the same door where in we went. Did we start with an immediate fact of consciousness and construct a world? Then let us now begin with the world and construct an immediate fact of consciousness.

To be sure, the familiar scenes of the journey in will look altered on the way out, but isn't that rather what we had hoped for? At all events, it is vain to cry paradox at each new episode of the kind. For example, we came to grief by assuming a man to know his own mind better any anything else and prior to anything else in the world. Somewhere along the way out we should expect to run across the reflection that his own mind is the last thing a man comes to know. "It is so far from self-evident," I had ventured to write, "that each man's mental state is his own indisputable possession, no one hesitates to confess at times that his neighbor has read him better than he has read himself. . . . No one finds fault with Thackeray for intimating that the old Major is a better judge of Pendennis's feeling for the Fotheringay than is Pendennis himself."

Mr. Miller selects the passage for an illustration of his difficulties:

> This is not a question of knowing our feelings, but of knowing how our feelings will develop or continue. To have a feeling and to be acquainted with it are the same thing. If a man does not know whether he is in love, it means that he does not know whether what he actually feels is or is not a sign of a continued disposition to feel and to act such as goes under that name.

And again I had said, continuing the thought, "It is quite as likely that under certain conditions I do not know what red is, as that under other conditions I do not know what love is."

But "this," comments Mr. Miller, "is not a question whether I am acquainted with my own sensation, but whether I am acquainted with the social name for my sensation."

These are only moments of our progress; but Mr. Miller is right in choosing them to illustrate a difference of view that must go with every step we take together. I wish indeed he had put his first objection a trifle differently. Unless love is of its essence enduring, there was no question of what Pendennis's feeling would develop into; still less would I have chosen Pen as an example of one who "did not know whether he was in love." I assumed that we were dealing with a man who was "sure" he was in love—later, with a man who was "sure" he saw the color red. Were they right or wrong in their surety? Or rather, has the question, Were they right or wrong? a meaning?

My own position: The question has so much meaning that it takes all the science of all the world to make out whether A is in love or whether B sees red. In that science A and B have their little part—they are contributors of undetermined value —but that they have the supreme, the ultimate part seems to me an assumption as little warranted as to suppose that I know better than all the world the nature of the pen I am holding because, forsooth, it is mine. Is it only a matter of the "social name" for the state of mind each surely has? Is it only that this one may err in calling his feeling "love," that one in calling his "red"? Then may they not err in calling their respective feelings by any other names, or by any names at all? And what should we, the philosophers, call that which maybe isn't this and maybe isn't that, but surely *is* the immediate and certain possession of the one who has it? "What shall we call that which can have no name?" Isn't the shade of Protagoras whispering something about "the last seeming"? Isn't Gorgias nudging my elbow? Isn't Cratylus congratulating himself on having held his peace and but wagged his finger?

However, enough of episodes! The general idea is that we start with a world and construct an immediate fact of consciousness. If this is the problem, we might be expected sooner or later to ask ourselves, What beings of this world do we call conscious, and why do we call them so? Is not this a search for the *meaning* of consciousness? It seemed to me that there must be something peculiar in the behavior of "conscious" beings, the which, if I could discover it, would give me the definition I sought. Their "consciousness" is that trait of the behavior of certain objects which makes me call them conscious; their "life," that trait which makes me call them alive; their "heat," that trait which makes me call them hot—so I thought one might argue.

Mr. Miller does not complain of me (I think?) for having attempted no more than this *statement* of an experimental problem. His objection is to the statement itself.

> Once more [he asks] the question what leads me to call a man conscious, and the question what consciousness means—is Mr. Singer assuming that they are the same question? Are the nature of a thing and the tokens by which I infer its presence the same? . . .

They are to me the same: I confuse, I identify the question, What leads me to call a man conscious? with the question, What does consciousness mean? And I detect in myself the same lack of intellectual scruples in other situations. I am inclined to confuse the question, What leads me to call this thing a triangle? with the question, What does triangle mean? Whether it is that I have wearied me of common-sense, or that my logic has lost its pertinacity, I cannot see why I should treat a conscious being more befoggedly than a triangle. Is making a mystery of them a way of paying tribute to the "higher categories"?

In watching the behavior of beings I call by instinct "conscious" (the reason for which instinct constitutes my problem) I seem to find grounds for differentiating this part of their behavior into "faculties." Among other faculties, I attribute to them "sensibility."[1] Part of their action I call "reaction"; I call it their seeing of a color, their hearing of a sound. As my experience of other minds grows, my knowledge of my own is enriched: I class myself among those who see and hear. Further, I recognize certain behavior as *descriptive*, and notice the way in which descriptive behavior varies with the conditions governing seeing and hearing. All do not see the same thing or see the same thing in the same way. Mr. Miller makes much of this difference of content as a peculiarity—yes, as the very essence—of our notion of consciousness.

The reasons why we say we find something in the world of facts which we call consciousness and which distinguishes itself from a behaving body [Mr. Singer] really does not consider. These reasons are after all simple.. . . . Let us try to state the reasons without the terms of personality, self, etc. For example, at a single moment a certain number of objects . . . are in a

[1] *Vid.* p. 77 sqq., ''On Sensibility.''

peculiar sense *together,* while those objects and other objects are not in the same sense together. . . . Of course the easiest way of putting this is to say *I am seeing* the first mentioned combination and *I am not seeing* [the second]. But it is quite easy to avoid making these references to self and its ''seeing'': it is quite easy to put it in terms of the ''objective'' facts themselves. These facts have a way of being *together,* some of them, while others are not in this sense together. . . . Groups there are, and breaches between them there are. Consciousness there is, and oblivion there is.

Ungefähr sagt das der Pfarrer auch—but with a slightly different meaning! For Mr. Miller concludes:

''Consciousness'' here is not behavior; it is, according to usage, either the ''field'' itself or the relation of conjunction between the components of the field.

It cannot be as a concession to my manner of speaking that Mr. Miller would avoid the easiest way of putting things. It is not I who object to such phrases as "*I am seeing* the rug" and "*I am not seeing* the window," or again "*I* am seeing the rug and *he* is seeing the window." As I arrive through observation at the notion of descriptive behavior, discover the way in which this varies with the point of view, I quite come to recognize that I see different things at different times; that I and another see different things at the same time. From this I gradually struggle toward an understanding of what is the same in the thing we so differently see, of the "objective" and the "subjective" factors in every description. I come to discover a subjective factor in my account of the very world with which I started. I come to see that the purely objective world and the purely subjective datum of consciousness are two ideals toward which we endlessly strive, modifying our notions of each as we change our understanding of the other.

Are there not left vestiges of sanity, even of something like common-sense, in my simple philosophy? Who has ever been offered an immediate state of consciousness out of which to construct a world? Who has not been forced to start with a world, which it was his given task to *re*construct? It is only in this process of reconstruction that the concepts of "consciousness" and "object of consciousness" fall out—*they fall out together*, and together they grow apace. To follow the adventures of this pair is, I suspect, to be led deep into the heart of things.[1]

[1] *Cf.* p. 183 sq.

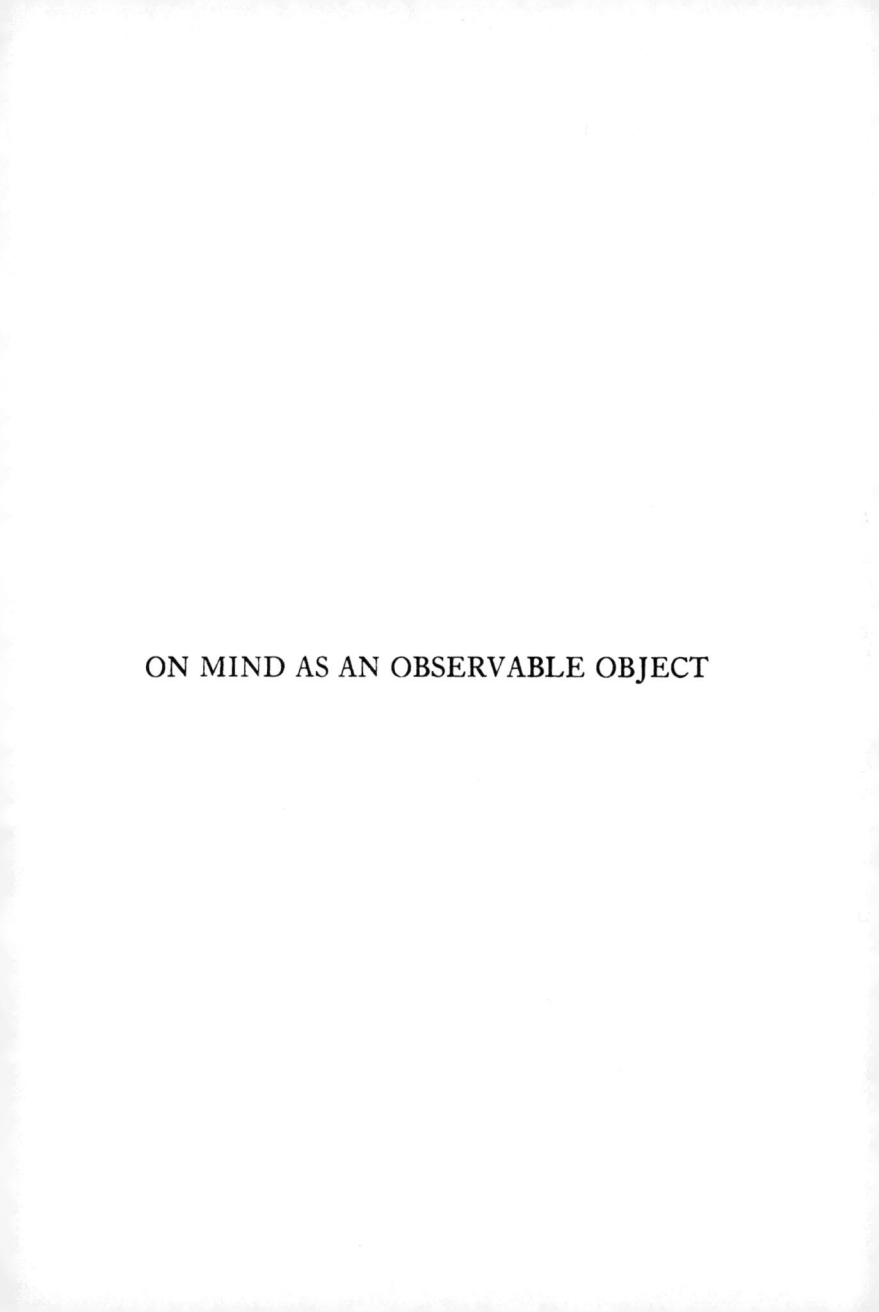

ON MIND AS AN OBSERVABLE OBJECT

III.

ON MIND AS AN OBSERVABLE OBJECT[1]

A PAPER of this same title which I offered a year ago met with a success beyond my expectation. It is something to have aimed at brevity and to be assured one has not missed completeness. Now there are a number of ways in which a theory of mind may be vitally amiss: in its epistemological background, in its psychological application, in its ethical consequences. Yet brief as was my exposition, my critics gave me to understand that I had let none of these ways of going astray escape me.

If then I return to my thesis, if I am led into an insistence neither justified by its merit nor excused by its interest, something must be forgiven a scruple: I would make sure that my sinning was as round and perfect as my critics would have me think.

As for background, it cannot be painted in with a word or two. Professor Miller in the *Journal of Philosophy* has called attention to the defects of an epistemology that would let one speak of mind as a trait of behavior, and I have met as best I could objections so well considered and so clearly put.

[1] Paper prepared to be read before the Philosophical Association at Cambridge, December, 1911.

ON MIND AS AN OBSERVABLE OBJECT

This matter of background may then be allowed to rest for the moment, but it is with no little regret that I postpone the consideration of ethical consequences. For I was greatly interested in a criticism of Professor Ormond's making: One who regards mind as a trait of behavior, must he not hold that when the body is dissolved in death the soul that once inspired its outworn flesh is also dissipated and lost?

I have spoken too hastily of criticism. Mr. Ormond would justly blame me for classing under this head remarks that were meant for no more than question. Mr. Ormond would be no more inclined than I to assume that a philosopher is bound to save his soul. On the other hand, I am at least as unwilling as Mr. Ormond could be to divest myself of any rag of immortality that may still cling to me in this cool age. But there are immortal souls and immortal souls. The learned in their high power of abstraction have pretended to find solace in the thought of a soul that, surviving the body, continues to enjoy all the individuality embodiment once conferred on it; living on, I know not where; experiencing, I know not what—I can't think how. This very algebraic soul, this diagram of an ethical idea, my thought may inadvertently have rubbed out. If so, let that rest which never has rested.

But simple folk too have their notion of immortality, and with the simple I would seem to have much in common. I should be sorry to feel that nowhere in my philosophy might I come across the like of that brave and kind soul which has gone "marching on" now these many years in the songs that men sing. Would you say that my thought had fallen into undignified ways if it sought this spirit in the very world that still sings its name, in the world which still holds a grave where its body "lies a-mouldering"?

Of all these delicate, difficult matters I would willingly speak another time. Just now there faces me an issue more vital than the destiny of souls after death—it has to do with the nature of souls during life.

To Miss Washburn, whose interest lies in comparing souls, I am indebted for a criticism that cared little enough what theory of knowledge may have gone before my thesis, what ethics might follow on it. Miss Washburn's criticism aimed at things practical: What are you going to do with a being who thinks, but who exhibits no behavior for the very reason that he thinks? What are you going to do with the passive, the utterly passive thinker?

Before the Panthéon at Paris sits Rodin's image of The Thinker. I know that a statue doesn't really think, but I know too that those who think may sit as stonily statuesque as Rodin's Thinker. Of one who has dared to suggest that mind is a trait of behavior it must inevitably be asked, What in the behavior of the thinker who doesn't behave is his thought?

In the face of criticism so sympathetic and yet so thoroughgoing, it would be vain to point out the differences that make flesh not marble and marble not flesh. Of course the creature of blood and muscle is not wholly inert: his heart beats, he breathes, his eyes blink. More than that—the dendronated termini of the axis-cylinder processes of his cortical nerve-cells may now and then put forth a new shoot; at the very least, some molecules of him may effect an interchange of atoms while he thinks. The trouble is that Miss Washburn refuses to identify any sort of a motion of atoms with a thought, and this makes the whole situation trying. If I say that the movement of certain atoms is what I mean by the behavior which is thought, the hands of Vogt and Büchner will reach out from Orcus and have me. If I refuse to say this, my own hands will seem to cast me off.

One who has to surmount an obstacle of magnitude is entitled, is he not, to a running start? a start from old and settled things if any such can be found that hold an analogy? Now this image of the passive thinker does suggest to me something so old as to be almost forgotten—it is the figure of "dormant life."

In the *British Foreign Medical Review* for January, 1839, appears the review of a recent medical work. The author, Mr. Carpenter, had defined life as *action* and had shown—so the sympathetic reviewer sums him up—"that instead of looking for its cause in an imaginary vital principle. . . . presumed to exist for the sake of explaining the phenomena, we ought to study the properties which organized structure enjoys and the agents which produce their manifestation."

Even to this reviewer of 1839 the idea that life is behavior has nothing new about it; for he continues, "Some observations are made [by Mr. Carpenter] in refutation of the doctrine of a vital principle and we do not think them supererogatory; for although the hypothesis would hardly have been expected to survive the fine scientific thrusts of Dr. Pritchard's classic weapon or the strokes of Dr. Fletcher's more truculent blade, it seems even yet not quite extinct."[1]

The theory that life was something other than behavior was not quite extinct in 1839! Will any theory that substitutes a *Ding an sich* for observable

[1] M. Paine, *Med. and Phys. Com.*, I., 13.

phenomena ever win to extinction? After dormant life comes passive thought.

But to return to 1839 and the years that follow. Among our early American physiologists is to be numbered Martyn Paine, whose work is characterized by the late Dr. Gross as "of great scope and much erudition." Of much erudition, surely, and I beg to recommend Paine's "Medical and Physiological Commentaries" to any in search of sources for a history of vitalism. Of what scope too I know to my sorrow. And yet of the pages and pages of erudition and scope would you know the one image that sticks firmly in my mind, Martyn Paine's arm and shield against classic weapon and truculent blade? It is just a seed, just an ordinary grain of corn, say. For one may defy the world to prove that this little dried-up thing is doing aught to support the hypothesis that it is alive. Yet one may take testimony of all the world that it is a living thing. Dormant life! What does it mean? It takes more than classic weapon and truculent blade to establish life as the thing Bichat defined it to be, "the *ensemble* of functions that resist death." There is the seed-corn that refuses to function, refuses to resist—for what is there to resist?—and yet it lives! But what in it is its life? Ah, it is a certain principle called "vital," dormant now, but only awaiting the right conditions to wake into the free gesture of life; into the blade, the ear, the full corn in the ear.

So Martyn Paine. But is it hard for us, who are not of 1839 or 1840, to see that the desiccated seed-corn is living not for what it does, if it does aught in a faint-hearted way to resist death, but just for what it might do? It is still on account of its doing that we call it alive; but on account of its prospective, not of its actual doing. It is *now* alive, for we may now calculate from its condition what under other conditions it would do.

If there is any analogy between dormant life and passive thinking I take some comfort in the formula in which my thesis was presented. Consciousness is behavior, if you will, but "more accurately, our belief in consciousness is an expectation of probable behavior based on an observation of actual behavior; a belief to be confirmed or refuted by more observation, as any other belief in a fact is to be tried out."

If Martyn Paine had so viewed dormant life, he would not have felt the need of appealing to a vital principle. He would not have added this unobservable thing to facts observable, in order to explain the meaning of the terms we use in describing these facts. If we can bring ourselves to view the passive thinker as we view passive life, we shall not have to add an "eject" or "thing-in-itself" to the behavior we see in him, in order to explain what more than this meager behavior is the rich thought we attribute to him. We shall perhaps find that what we add to behavior actually observed is an actual calculus of probabilities; but the nature of this calculus demands the nicest analysis both as to the grounds on which it rests and as to the kind of test to which it can ultimately be put.[1]

To come at the matter from another angle: the analogy argument for other minds would not be so pernicious if it were not so true. It offers an accurate account of what I do when I furnish a passive thinker's mind for him; only it fails to suggest any grounds on whch I may justify my doing; it avoids pointing out a way by which I may discover a mistake if I have made one or enjoy the sense of truth if I have hit on it.

Yonder, say, is my thinker. It is of course the observation of past and present behavior that invites me to consider him as a thinker at all, and may even suggest to me that his thought is dwelling on a mathematical problem. But sooner or later in defining his thought I venture a leap in the dark—fill his mind with the kind of thing that goes on in mine. I am not justified by observation, but since I know that a mathematician cannot think

[1] *Cf.* p. 91, "virtual" behavior.

about mathematics in the abstract I give him a definite problem. He is trying to integrate a differential equation; now he has seized upon a transformation that looks promising; for a moment he hopes, in another moment he has cast the suggestion aside —it has not worked. One may elaborate to one's taste, one is still abstract while the fact before one must be concrete. Our mathematician is integrating? Very well, what is he integrating? Is it an equation of the third order and fourth degree, or of the fourth order and third degree, or of some other order and some other degree?

The obvious resource of one who wants to know is to ask the thinker what he is thinking about. Whereupon the obvious remark of one who regards consciousness as expected behavior is that one who so asks is appealing to behavior to confirm or refute his expectation. But such a triumph is brief. The man who replies is already other than the man who thought. He is in a more advantageous position than I to venture a guess, in the same sense that he is better placed than I to see the wall behind my head; but for him as for me it is only a guess. Memory is generally less fallible than divination, but it is fallible enough. Meanwhile if the question as to this thinker's past has a meaning it has also an answer and there is a definable method of arriving at this answer or at least of indefinitely

ON MIND AS AN OBSERVABLE OBJECT

approximating to it. An appeal to the thinker to tell us what was his thought cannot give us the truth nor open a way by which we may approach the truth. The thought just past is lost in the infinite ocean of the past, the pebble just now dropped into this ocean is no easier of recovery than is the treasure sunk there a thousand years ago.

Let us then merge our present problem in a more general one; let us try to solve the difficult in terms of the more difficult; let us substitute for our passive thinker another hero.

From a certain letter of his, I judge that George Washington spent Christmas Day, 1798, at Mount Vernon. That there was a George Washington and that he was in a certain neighborhood at a certain past time, an examination of now existing things will enable me to establish. But what of his slave-boy, Cæsar? Was there such a slave-boy? At noon of this day was he in the kitchen of Mount Vernon helping the cook? And what was going through his mind at the moment? Was or wasn't it a thought of approaching dinner?

These questions, humble in themselves, acquire an immense dignity when we realize that it tasks all our philosophy to answer them. Yet there must be a way of answering such questions, or else there is in the domain of reality such a thing as an unknowable fact. This is an equally portentous figure to introduce into one's philosophy, whether it stand for the being and thought of a slave, or whether it be taken for the hidden name of God. In either meaning, in all meanings, it is a term I have long decided to leave out of my philosophy.[1] The right to do so is one of those questions of background with which I am not on this occasion dealing.

For me, then, and for all who so far agree with me, there must be a way of reconstructing the past. Now the only way of reconstructing the past which science has so far developed is suggested by the classic saying of Laplace: Give me the mass, position, and velocity of every particle of matter in the universe, and I will predict its future and recount its past. I say this utterance of Laplace suggests a method of reconstruction: it does not define one; he existed at a moment of the history of mechanics that took too seriously the conception of law at which it happened to have arrived. Of the refinements and generalizations that would have to be introduced in order to convert this suggestion into a definition, I have treated elsewhere, and as they do not affect the issue with which we are now dealing I shall pretend to take Laplace quite seriously.[2]

[1] *Vid.* p. 267 sqq., ''Kant's First Antinomy.''
[2] *Vid.* p. 231.

ON MIND AS AN OBSERVABLE OBJECT

If we do take such ideas seriously, we realize that the conditions on which the whole past may be reconstructed can never be realized. The data Laplace asks for is infinite, the law by which he pretends to handle this data is a law known to hold only within limits of a probable error which can never be reduced to zero. But what is interesting in the situation is that we can see no obstacle to the gathering of more and more of the data demanded, nor to the endless reduction of the probable error attaching to any law in which we propose to substitute the data gathered.

We have here then a method of approximating indefinitely a certain order of facts; but alas! it seems to be an order very different from that in which lay the facts about which we enquired. We asked, Did such a being live? Did he have such and such a thought? And we are answered, At least you may find out within any degree of accuracy required what atoms were in the neighborhood at the time you mention and how they were moving.

I was asked at the outset, Is the movement of an atom a thought? I was afraid to answer *yes*, and I was afraid to answer *no*. But such courage has come to me with study that I am now prepared to answer, *yes and no*. In order that this answer may not seem in any way ambiguous or evasive, I must explain that the movement of an atom is the movement of an atom and a thousand things beside.

> When my love swears that she is made of truth
> I do believe her though I know she lies.

As these lines passed for the first time through the poet's mind, I am ready to believe any Laplace who tells me that an atom of carbon in the poet's brain described such a such a path. But if the same reconstructor assured me that another atom of carbon, more like the first than one pea is like another, described just such another path as a certain lump of coal was being shot into my bin, I know not how I should disbelieve him. What then? If moving atoms are thoughts, had not that lump of coal a bit of the poet in its make up?

Love, as our poet sings it, is not the only god that teaches the ear to be willing and the heart to accept truths it knows to be untrue. Mathematical science with its beautiful simplicity has a way of casting spells as deep. The lust for mechanical images is as seductive to the intellect as are other desires to the flesh. One may laugh, but one may not by laughing cure. William James pointed out that the most ravishing music was *after all* but the rasping of hairs from a horse's tail on the intestines of a cat. Plato, with gentler irony, had the Socrates of his Phædo explain his situation in like terms. Why was he sitting there awaiting the cup, instead of flying to Megara or Bœotia? *After all* it was because his bones were at a certain angle with each other and his muscles drawn in such a way as to keep them so.

Such sayings as these would be without humor if they were not true. There is nothing false in any of them—or at least there is nothing more false than the recurrent "after all" which seems merely to introduce them. However, nothing can belie a truth as can the gesture with which it is presented. Granted that the poet, the musician, the moral being, is a congeries of moving atoms, is he *after all* nothing more? Cossmann in his *Empirische Teleologie* has a way of answering the question which has always seemed to me full of meaning. Because, he says, mechanism is *allgültig* it is not therefor *alleingültig*. Mechanical insights give the truth, they only deceive us when we take this to be the whole truth.

Now the vice of those who in the past have criticized the view that would treat mind as an aspect of mechanical behavior is that the critics themselves have been the slaves of mechanical and mathematical ideas. They have seen that there is a sense in which the movement of atoms taking place in a body can not be the thought of that body viewed as a thinker. They have proceeded with the instinct of a mathematician to add something; just as a cook whose dish is tasteless adds seasoning. But as they couldn't get the right flavor by adding more atomic movements, they added an "eject," a "parallel series," an "epiphenomenon."

My whole suggestion is that instead of helping out the shortcomings of a mechanical description of experience by the mechanical addition of something not falling within experience, we simply change our point of view toward the mechanism with which we are presented when that mechanism *also* behaves in a teleological way. Then we shall not be tempted, in trying to say what the movement of a certain atom of carbon has to do with Shakespeare's thought, to study its analogy with all similar movements of atoms of carbon in the wide world. If we insist on doing this, we cannot fail to arrive at the conclusion that such movements as a class have nothing to do with thoughts as a class. But then, if in order to learn what the turning of a certain wheel in my watch had to do with keeping time, I compared it with all the wheels in the world (those of locomotives, those of rapid-fire artillery, and the rest), I should have to conclude that wheels as a class have on the whole nothing to do with chronometry.

I come back at last to my passive thinker. What I observe of his present behavior is not his thought; what I expect in the way of future behavior is not the full meaning of his thought, even though that behavior be a minute exposition on his part of what he *believes* to have been his thought; what I might observe of the minutest mechanical changes in him is or is not his thought, as I view it. Detail by detail these atomic movements may be classed with other atomic movements whose class has no common function. Putting all together—all that are contained within his skin—I should think it unlikely that if they occurred within another skin placed in other surroundings they would work the same ends, be essential to the same activity of mind. But in so far as they are the mechanism by which the same peculiar aspect of teleological behavior may elsewhere be worked out—then I am willing to say, This is the behavior of the passive thinker that I mean by his thought.[1] I should begin by looking for such movements of atoms as actually moved

---

[1] That is, these are the only events in space and time that place the thought in history. The non-mechanical classification of these events leads to a new order of expectancy. This, their teleological, is also their psychological interpretation. *Vid.* p. 89 sqq. "On Sensibility."

ON MIND AS AN OBSERVABLE OBJECT

(too slightly for us to notice it) the organs of expression: the tongue, principally, and the eyes. Or perhaps I should find part of the movements to be of this nature, part of them such as strained the muscles that inhibited such expression. Either would be the first step toward a teleological interpretation of a mechanical event. But of these details I am not sure. To find just what that behavior is which others call the criterion of mind and which I call mind is a problem of long and careful analysis. For this analysis we must turn to the psychologist, and, above all, I have recently come to hope, to the comparative psychologist. Yet even this hope must learn to be patient. When one passes beyond new observations to look for new interpretations one finds the shadow of the "eject" clouding fresh fields:

"Bien entendu," writes Georges Bohn in a chapter discussing the "criteria of psychism"[1]—"bien entendu, je ne parlerai pas ici de la conscience des animaux. Je ne la nie pas, mais je ne peux rien savoir à son égard. Je parlerai de psychisme, ce mot designant la complexité de phénomènes que je parviens à analyser plus ou moins."

I can not think a metaphysics useless that might prevent a writer of the keen intelligence of M. Bohn from perverting his own sense of what words should

[1] *Naissance de l'Intelligence,* p. 111.

mean to the use of those whom he occasionally refers to as "metaphysicians." In science as elsewhere, it is not a bad thing to have one's courage with one; and a very little, I should think, would suffice to "deny" what one "will not speak of"—what one cannot speak of for the simple reason that one can know nothing about it. Isn't it saner to seek the meaning of consciousness itself among "the phenomena one can more or less analyze"?

THE PULSE OF LIFE

IV.

THE PULSE OF LIFE

On various occasions I have expressed the opinion that life and mind must be defined in terms of behavior, whether observed or expected. The reasons that led me to this conclusion have been set forth at sufficient length,—they all come back to this one: that to assert the existence or non-existence of any thing is meaningless unless we can verify the assertion. But experience is the only means of verifying assertions, and behavior the only aspect of the beings we call living or conscious which is matter for experience. Hence in our empirical reasons for calling one thing alive, another not, one thing conscious, another unconscious, must lie the meaning of life and mind.

I had not thought to return to this matter whose interest for me lay rather in what it led up to than in its own modest content. But I have come to see that one cannot define a method without illustrating it, unless one is willing to be widely misunderstood. I have had sufficient occasion to realize this, for the thesis which seemed to me so much a matter of course has been regarded by many as revolutionary, not to say *"waghalsig,"* [1] and a way of looking at things which I should have called Aristotelian has been interpreted as "materialistic." [2]

The fault, of course, is my own. I have confined myself to showing why life and mind *must* be defined by a certain method, and have offered no reply to those who ask,—But how *can* they be? I have pointed to behavior as that in terms of which life and mind must be set forth, but I have not answered the question,—What behavior? To be sure,

> *Kein tolleres Versehen kann sein*
> *Giebst einem ein Fest und lädst ihn nicht ein.*

To mend all this there is but one way, and that is to sketch-in a picture of the world as it appears to one who has come to look upon life and mind as behavior. Such a picture cannot be presented with any confidence that its details are correctly drawn; as one hand moves the pencil the other is ready with the eraser. But as an illustration of method the whole imperfect thing has its interest, and while in my impatience to get on to the consequences of a theory I faced the task of illustrating it as an unwelcome interruption, I have nevertheless experienced in the working-out no little enjoyment.

[1] Jacoby, *Internationale Monatsschrift*. Jg. 8, No. 1, p. 7.
[2] Montague, "The New Realism," p. 271.

But in this first paper I shall attempt no more than a picture in which *life* appears—the concept of *mind* shall be for another time.

Life and Mechanism

As the medium in which the image of life is to be wrought, let me assume the world of mechanism. When I conceive such a world, I spread it out in space and attach to each of its points a limited number of characteristics or parameters which I then connect by such formulas as enable me to express their values as functions of a single variable, *time*. To construct such an image of the world we live in is the ideal of physical science. It is only an ideal, and to have chosen it as a medium in which to work means no more than to have registered a pious intent to introduce no definition of life or mind which shall stop our approach to the mechanical ideal. Those whom the history of physical science inspires with no such respect for its ideal as to require them to conform their notions of life to it will care little for an image worked out in a medium they reject. Their quarrel with me is serious enough; but this is not the moment to enter on it nor a suitable *terrain*. It can be only for such as regard the mechanical ideal as inviolable that the problem of defining life consistently with it is a real problem.[1]

[1] *Cf.* p. 227 spp., "On Mechanical Explanation."

But for such the problem is very real; for every one knows how difficult it is to pass from an image of the world as mechanism to an understanding of that same world as the medium not only in which, but also of which life has its being. The difficulty which this transition offers to thought has sometimes been taken for a very hiatus in the order of nature, a chasm and an abyss so threatening to the continuity—not to say the consistency—of our thought that the most extraordinary philosophies have been built to bridge it. The most notorious of these inventions are (1) that which attempts to make life consistent with mechanism by making life mechanical, (2) that which tries to make mechanism consistent with life by making mechanism alive at every point. The first, I think,[1] may fairly be called a *materialistic*, the second a *monadistic* account of the relation of life to mechanism.

For one who confines himself to determining what behavior on the part of certain objects of our experience makes us call them living, and who then defines life as that which is common to the behavior

---

[1] I say "I think," for since I find that I have myself been called a "panhylist," which must be an aggravated variety of materialist, I am not sure that I know what idea, if any, the term *materialist* conveys. If every one is a materialist who refuses to look upon the contours of a living being as the boundary of a region in which the kind of predictability that holds outside of it breaks down, then I am a materialist along with Spinoza and Kant. If, on the other hand, a materialist is one who attempts to give a mechanical definition of life, then, unlike Democritus or Lamettrie, I am no materialist.

of living things, neither materialism nor monadism is possible; but neither for such an one does the gap exist for whose bridging these philosophies have been invented. He makes it his problem so to define life that it may dwell in mechanism and be of it, but in such manner that neither shall life be turned into mechanism nor mechanism into life.

Materialism

In framing such a definition of life we shall be in accord with very old tradition if we consider that a certain purpose is revealed in the behavior of the beings we call living, and that it is because of this purposive behavior we call them so. But to erect this purpose into a definition of life is to enter at once on the troubled domain of teleological definition.

The confusion usually attendant on this method of defining comes, I think, from our failure to keep distinct the two classes into which a single individual may fall when one of these classes is defined without reference to purpose; the other connotes nothing but a sameness of purpose. The distinction is obvious enough when our thought is not troubled by the application of both methods of classifying to the same object. The classes "triangle," "gravitational system," "salt" suggest nothing of a common purpose served by triangles, or by gravitational systems, or by salts. A triangle *must be* three-sided and plane; it *may be* the best form for a spear-head, for an element of a bridge-truss, for a certain fashion of musical instrument. Neither is any one purpose served by gravitational systems, nor have salts a unique function. The definition of these geometrical, physical, and chemical concepts is ateleological; and the sciences dealing with terms so defined might be called *ateleological sciences*. On the other hand, the classes "musical instrument," "time-piece," "seasoning" connote nothing of the geometry, physics, or chemistry of the subjects contained in them. A musical instrument *must be* capable of producing pleasant tones; it *may have* the structure of a triangle, or of a fiddle, or of a flute. So "time-pieces" may vary in mechanism from a sun-dial to a chronoscope, and to make its proper appeal the "seasoning" may call for salt or it may call for pepper. If, then, there is any group of sciences whose peculiar and specific concepts are defined in terms of purpose and place no limit on the variety of mechanisms which may be found to serve this purpose, we might call such sciences *teleological*. It is in this group we should place biology, if that *life* of which biology is the study is properly defined in terms of purpose alone.

No one would be tempted to confuse these two *principia divisionis* if it were not for the puzzling way in which the classes they denote intersect and overlap. For example, that portion of the extended world which is at this moment bounded by the surface of my body is part of the universal mechanism, and is more or less like other parts in its mechanical structure. Hence it belongs to a class of mechanisms, ateleologically defined. Am I not, then, a machine? On the other hand, the history of my body's behavior reveals a purpose running through its various acts, a purpose quite like that which characterizes my neighbor, my dog, the moth that flutters by me. Am I not then a being with a purpose? And one may repeat this question apropos of every member of the class "living-being": it is a member of that class because its behavior reveals purpose; it has at each moment membership in another class defined without reference to purpose. Which is it, *really*, a thing of purpose or a mechanism?

But the question answers itself, and I introduce it merely to point out the part it plays in the psychology of materialism. For materialism is nothing but an attempt to define life in terms of mechanism. It observes correctly enough that each living thing has at each moment a place in a class of mechanisms: it fails to observe how endlessly unlike these classes may be, and seeks to state what is common to them as the definition of *life*. But there is nothing in the way of mechanism common to all that is or might be called living, and the living would never be put into a single class were they not moments in a scheme of purpose: the class *living-being* has nothing but a certain purpose common to its members, and only this purpose can be offered as the definition of life. It is for this reason that as living I am classed with the grass of the field: as mechanism I am much more like my own corpse.

Monadism

If the definition of life as a certain kind of purposeful behavior makes materialism impossible, it makes "monadism" or "hylozoism" no less so. For implicit in the concept of purpose is that of freedom, and freedom is exactly that which we have denied to the points of our mechanical system. At the point there can be no freedom, no purpose, no life.

That freedom is implicit in our definition of life may be made to appear by either of two comparisons. If we follow the history of any individual living thing we observe through what varying mechanical vicissitudes (of light, heat, chemism) it works out its purpose, "adapting itself" as we say to a wider or narrower range of circumstance. Or if we compare, not the same individual at different moments, but the most resemblant individuals at the same moment, we may measure their adaptability in terms of the range of mechanical situations that leaves their purpose as living beings undefeated. But to accomplish the same defining purpose in a variety of mechanical situations is to be independent of mechanism to a degree measured by the range of things that "do not matter."

The invariance of purpose in a variety of mechanical situations is freedom. We do not first find life and then speculate as to the freedom of living beings; it is not until we have found this freedom that we are sure of having found life.[1]

It is clear then that in a system whose points are assumed to be mechanically connected we can not posit life in all its freedom *at the point*. The only remaining posibility is to regard life as a phenomenon of the *group of points*. But how are we to effect a grouping of mechanically determined points so that the group shall be free when the points are not? How can a kind of grouping introduce freedom into a system whose elements are not free?

Theory of the "Pulse"

The relation of whole to part is no one relation, but presents an infinite variety. The simplest type

[1] Curiously enough the attention of those who discuss "freedom" has been centered on the possibility of doing different things under the same circumstances. This is not freedom, but caprice. Our freedom is measured by our ability to do the same thing under different circumstances: it is that *independence of circumstance* which Stoic and Epicurean understood so well.

is that in which the whole is said to be equal to the sum of its parts, and because of the ease and familiarity of the operation of adding we are only too willing to think of all grouping as summation and to apply to it the principles of arithmetic. As a matter of fact the examples which our experience offers us of what might be called additive groups are rare: we think of a foot as the sum of the inches comprising it, of a pound as the sum of the ounces contained in it; but we should not get very far if we tried to think of a chemical molecule as the sum of its atoms, and we should go much too far if we insisted upon defining a state as the sum of its citizens. At the outset, then, it is well to protect oneself against a natural tendency to apply axioms of addition to all forms of composition. Can it be less absurd to say, The whole being equal to the sum of its parts, if there is no freedom in the part there can be none in the whole, than to say, A triangle being composed of straight lines, if there is no triangularity about each of these lines there can be none in their combination? [1]

Now of all the ways of composing a whole out of parts there is none which holds more surprises in store for the arithmetical soul than that which permits us to regard a wave moving through a medium

[1] For historic illustrations, *cf.* "Modern Thinkers and Present Problems," the chapters: "Spinoza"; "A Disciple of Spinoza."

as made up of the parts of that medium itself; for in no other form of composition is the non-additive character of the grouping more obvious, in none other is the contradiction between the properties of the group and the properties of the elements grouped more keenly felt. Through a medium whose parts are moving up and down, a pulse composed of these very parts may move horizontally; through a medium whose parts are moving back and forth about a center of equilibrium, a pulse may pass on and on. If we have overcome the primitive instinct to add, if the peculiarities of wave-composition no longer surprise us, there can be nothing to shock us in the further suggestion that through a medium of mechanism all of whose points are determined, a pulse of life may pass freely on its way.

Following this suggestion our method of defining life, though it insists upon the distinction between mechanism and life, denies the chasm between them. For imagine that through the infinite sea of mechanism already defined, there move certain wave-like forms, not indeed wind-tossed, but rather purpose-drawn; and imagine the purpose in terms of which the behavior of these forms could be explained and predicted to be that of *self-preservation*; would not each of these pulses correspond in all respects to what we call a living thing? Is it not as such a pulse that each thing which lives moves slowly on through the vast sea of mechanism drawn this way and that, not as the waves of the ocean are blown, but as "the lover is moved by the loved object"—until breaking upon some sudden obstacle or dying out in the viscous medium it is seen no more? But between such a pulse of life and the universal mechanism in which it arises, through which it purposefully moves awhile and into which it passes away again, there is no discontinuity or break. A new thing has indeed appeared, a new thing that is not to be defined or studied by the methods of mechanics: this new thing is a *group*; a group which is in the nature of a *pulse*; a pulse whose behavior may be defined in terms of *purpose*; a purpose which we recognize to be that of *self-preservation*, requiring adjustment and adaptation to the various mechanical situations through which in the course of its history the pulse freely passes. This new thing is *life*.

The Science of Life

But if life can not be mechanically defined, if living behavior can not be mechanically explained or predicted, in what sense can there be a science of life? What must be the nature of the laws of such a science and on what sort of calculations can it enter?

The answer to these questions must depend upon our understanding of the term "purpose," which has entered into our definition of life and so must control our treatment of living phenomena.[1] I take it that the accomplished purpose of an act will always be sought among the results of that act. No doubt the chick yonder embodies the purpose for which a certain egg was laid: it is also a result of that laying. But if we were to follow all the results of that laying, a humble barnyard episode would turn into a cosmic event on our hands. For that egg in descending has jarred the universe, and one wonders why out of its endless consequences just this unimpressive chick should have been taken as the one for whose sake the event befell. What in the world distinguishes the result that is a purpose from the infinity of other consequences that are merely accidental?

I know how usual it is to define purpose as the *desired* result and to accommodate this definition as best one may to the purposeful acts of the humbler order of beings; to the tree whose blossoming must express some one's or some thing's desire for another tree of the same kind; to the unicellular organism whose ingesting of a foreign body must betray its hunger. But in order that the concept of desire may have so wide an extension, must we not

[1] *Cf.* p. 261 sqq., "On Final Causes."

have made its meaning identical with that of purpose? Must we not have offered a tautology in place of a definition? Or else we may have done worse than this. We may have made of desire some immediate experience of which we believe ourselves in possession, but of which we can give no account or description; we may then have trusted to luck in assuming that others would understand us when we used this term; we may finally have appealed to analogy to justify the hypothesis that all things acting purposefully have a like subjective experience. The emptiness of each phrase setting forth the process by which I am supposed to read my own inarticulate experiences into others has been sufficiently insisted upon elsewhere.[1] It will be well enough to point out at this time that no one could verify the "hypothesis" of desire in fellow-man, fowl, shrub, or amœba. How then could one make use of these unknown desires to distinguish the known purpose of an act from its accidental results?

No, the definition of purpose can gain nothing by an appeal to desire as that which can be established first in the study of any given act and then used to distinguish the purpose of that act from its accidental consequences. Such an appeal does indeed suggest that the distinction between the pur-

[1] *Vid.* p. 3 sqq.

pose and the accidental results of a given act requires us to collect other data than that furnished by the mechanical description of the act and its consequences. But this data can only be collected if it is as observable as the act itself. And what can be as observable as the act, except another act that is like it? Here then we have our suggestion. If but once in the known history of the universe an egg were laid, a blossom burst, a morsel were ingested, would there be any possibility of our recognizing among the consequences of each unique event one that was its purpose? Or if the same sort of event happened many times, but among the consequences none were found to be common to the various cases, would we then be able to recognize a purpose in that type of event? But if, on the other hand, the type of event happened frequently enough to enable us to compare the spheres of consequence that emanated from each case as from an origin, and if we found that in a certain proportion of cases the same kind of result followed, would we not be justified in looking upon this *average common result* as *the purpose of the act*, assigning the remaining variable consequences to accident?[1]

Purpose then may be defined as the average common result of a type of act. As an average result it is not expected to follow "always" but only as

[1] *Vid.* p. 263.

Aristotle would say "for the most part." Or rather, this classic expression is still too vigorous. For we recognize a result as a purpose when it is common to but a very small percentage of the cases falling within the type of act whose purpose it is. The purpose of the depositing of each shad's egg is no doubt the production of another shad, but it would be unfortunate for the rest of us if this result followed for the most part on the event. In place of the loose Aristotelian phrase we should substitute an exact mathematical expression, one that is based on an empirical study of statistics and presents itself finally as a *measured probability*. We may say then that the purpose of an event is the result which that type of event is *calculated* to accomplish; the calculus in question having for its data statistics and for its method the theory of probabilties.

A teleological science has for its laws the statistical principles which we call rules, but to contrast it for this reason with the "exact" sciences is inexact. For though from the very nature of the concepts it employs a teleological science must deal with principles that apply to the individuals of a group *collectively*, and not *distributively*, there is no limit to the exactness with which these laws can be expressed. If we are interested in applying its results to an individual of a group it has studied, it can only offer us material for a calculus of what this individual will probably do, but it can give to this probability as exact an expression as it chooses.

There is then a science of life; it is an exact science of the probable in the domain of self-preservative behavior.

"Self-Preservation" Defined

It requires I suppose no special defense, that we have taken only one of the purposes revealed in the behavior of living beings as the *defining* purpose. Any self-preservative being may belong to a number of other teleological classes—the type-preservative for example. In general the possession of one "nature" by a given individual does not exclude the possession of a different and even contradictory nature; for from what has already been said respecting the meaning of teleological classification, it will appear that the behavior which justifies us in assigning an individual to a given class may be and generally is only part of its total behavior. It will not surprise us then if self-preservative beings are also type-preservative and if at moments their type-preservative acts are self-destructive. In framing our definition we have included in it only the minimal connotation that would give to the class defined the denotation which has been traditionally accorded to the term *life* and which we are prepared to preserve for future use. It is sufficient for us that no finite being devoid of self-preservative behavior has been called living, and that we are prepared to recognize as living a being, however constructed, however devoid of other purposes or natures, if only it reveal self-preservative behavior.

But is this concept of self-preservation itself so clear and well-defined that it may profitably serve for the defining of other terms? I confess that I am not one of those who move with ease and enjoyment through the domain of the reflexive categories. Even this most familiar one of self-preservation gives me pause. To preserve one's fortune, to preserve one's reputation, these expressions are intelligible enough because the preserver and the thing preserved are sufficiently marked-off the one from the other to permit of a relation being set up between them. But when the preserver and the preserved are as closely identified as one is with oneself, it is with no gaiety of heart that I approach the task of (Plato would say) so mixing "the same" with "the other" as to constitute the concept of self-preservation.

However, there comes to my mind the couplet into which a certain weary soul put the whole story of his life as it appeared to him in retrospect. "I ate," he said,

> "I ate, drank, slept, and then
> I ate, drank, and slept again."

Now whatever of the richness and variety sometimes pertaining to the lives of men this unimpressed person had managed to miss or to forget, he had not been able to leave untold a certain minimum which is the content of life itself. And this minimum seemed to him to consist in a precarious sort of *againness* whose monotonous rhythm had filled his years. If one had asked him why he had thus eaten, he would have said I fancy, in order that he might eat *again*. In the same sense that the fowl lays an egg in order to produce another fowl, our hero ate his dinner in order that he might eat another dinner. A being who so acts that the repetition of his act is well-calculated to result from it, whose act is seen to be a means of ensuring its recurrence, is a self-preservative being.

Such, at least, is the simplest life definable; but our hero's was relatively complex: he not only ate, but he also drank and slept. We should doubtless be too additive in our methods if we represented him as doing each of these things for the purpose of doing just that thing again. Did he not do each in order that he might do all three again? A in order that he might do A, B, C. . . . in the future, B, for the same reason, and C, with a like motive . . . ? A being whose acts may be analyzed into n types such that each type has for its purpose the repetition of all n types is not only a living being, but also an organism. I dare say we can find no example of a living being which is not also an organism, so that the terms living being and organism have come to be used interchangeably, but the meaning of organism contains more than the definition of life.

Thus we have our concept of organized self-preservation. The sameness implied in it is the sameness of the wave as a whole; the otherness, the rhythm of its complex and changing contour as it is transmitted by and translated through the medium in which and of which it is.

Concerning Death

With this definition of self-preservative behavior, the picture of life and its relation to mechanism is complete. Yet it may be a matter of surprise to some that we have included in our definition of life no reference to the episode of death, so universal as to be commonly regarded as a part of life itself. Even Professor Schaffer, who startled an over-excitable if not over-imaginative world by accepting the possibility of a laboratory creation of life, was unable to stretch his thought to the point of conceiving a laboratory prevention of death.[1] But if one has gone so far as to exclude from one's conception of living things all reference to their

[1] *Science*, N. S., 36, p. 289.

way of coming into being, it would seem natural that one should include in one's definition no reference to their manner of passing out again. The *possibility* of creating life and the *possibility* of eliminating death mean no more than that we may define life without reference to its beginning or end. Whether we can find or produce beings that fall within this definition and *also* meet certain conditions of beginning and ending is a purely empirical question, the ground of whose answering lies quite outside of the definition.

Birth and death then are only synthetically attached to life; but while the motive for reading birth into the definition of life is no deeper than an habitual association of ideas, I am not sure that the insistence on death as a thing whose germ lies in birth is to be explained in the same way. For we have seen that the teleological method of defining which gives us our concept of life is essentially statistical and looks upon the future of each thing in a class as a matter of probability. In order that there should be nothing more than probability, there must be a possibility that the future expected should not arrive: there must then be cases in which it does not. But the defeat of the purpose of the living being is death, and so its occurrence would seem to be essential to the meaning of life. It will be remarked, however, that this necessity of death is but a requirement that some die, not that all die. Death is an essential phenomenon of a group taken collectively, not of that group taken distributively. As for any individual, it is enough that for him life is not certain; nothing requires us to maintain that death is.

So I have defined life without reference to its beginning or its end; I have also defined it without reference to its higher and lower forms. It is possible to do this because so far as life goes the existence of the higher form is not involved in the meaning of the lower, and conversely. Where however these differences of higher and lower life exist, it is possible to introduce a new category to describe their relations. This new category is *mind*.

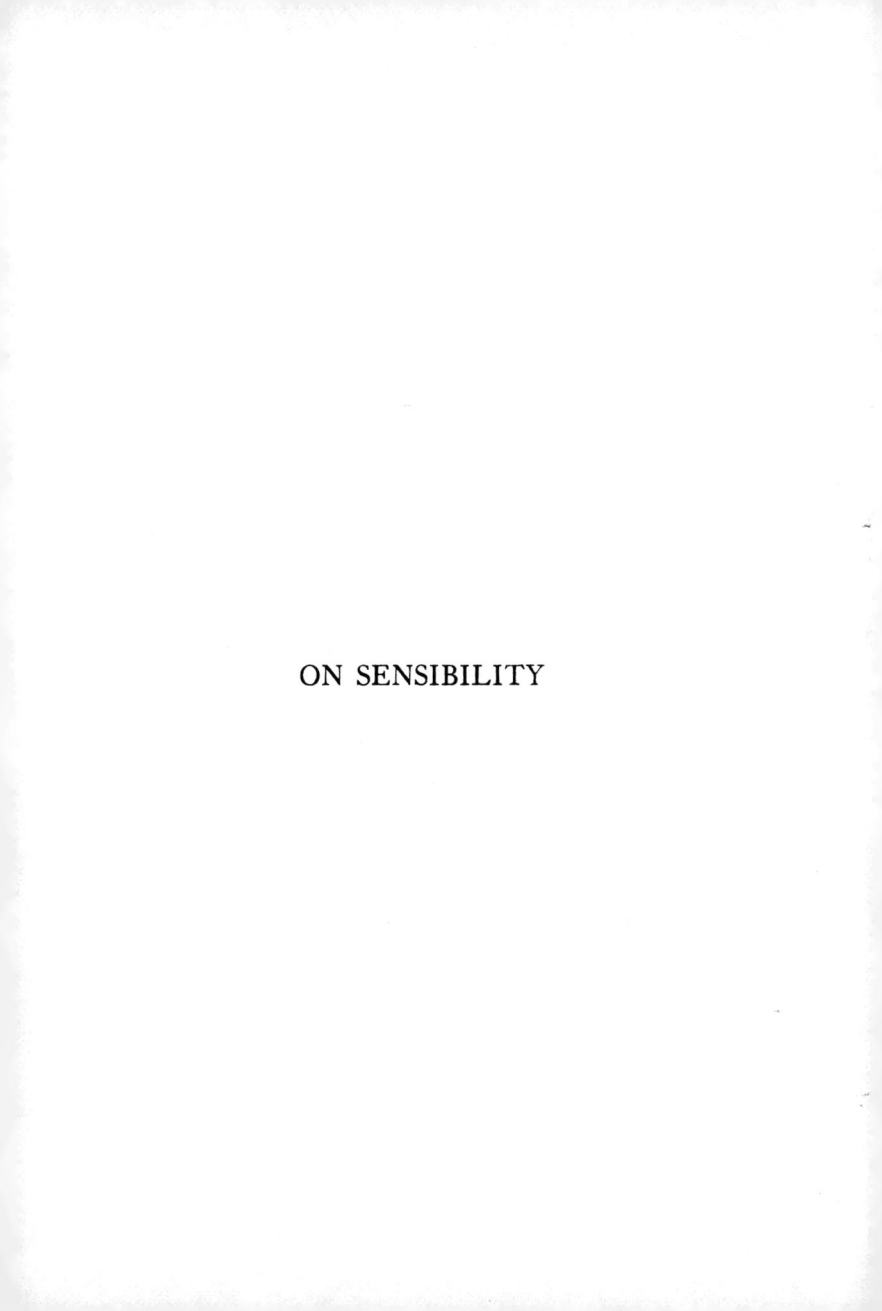

ON SENSIBILITY

V.

ON SENSIBILITY[1]

ONE who has tried to define *life*, with all its purposefulness and freedom, as a thing residing in and moving through mechanism without ceasing to be part of it, cannot be unacquainted with trouble. Yet, this task accomplished as best it might be, he would be innocent indeed who did not know that if he would go on to define *mind* in the same empirical way the worst of his perplexities lay before him. For to define a thing in an empirical or pragmatical way is so to define it as to leave no doubt what experiments would inform us whether anything corresponding to our definition existed or no. But where minds are concerned we have not yet or only recently grown scrupulous to avoid making hypotheses about them that suggest nothing in the way of an experiment by which our guesses might be tested. We have pretended to know too much of our own, been content to know too little or nothing at all of our fellow's mind; and empirical health is not in us. So that one to whom his own mind

[1] Paper written for the Philosophical Club of Columbia University, Spring of 1917.

is no immediate certainty and his neighbor's no unapproachable eject has trouble in explaining how and why both of them are objects to be experimented upon like trees or houses—and yet very unilke, too, in the kind of experiment they call for.

As these matters are not old and well-worn, but (if I may judge from the criticism previous papers of my own and of other sympathetic writers have called forth) new and even repugnant to prevailing habits of thought, there may be some advantage in beginning the discussion of them where otherwise one might rather have hoped to leave-off. A tentative generalization at the outset has often helped me, a reader, and I see no reason why the like should not be vouchsafed by me, a writer, if only it be not taken with too much finality. But if I start with some very loose reflections on the nature of mind, it will only be to abandon them as quickly as may be and to devote the body of my paper to one of the most special and technical problems with which an empirical method can be confronted.

"Mind" Required to Express Difference of Life

It will be remembered that the empirical method of defining mind begins by identifying what you would do to find out whether a being had a mind or not with what you mean by mind, or, as I have sometimes put it, "the criterion of mind constitutes its definition." Now those who have approached the problem of the criterion of mentality fall into two classes: some think they find mind wherever they find life and others attribute mind to only those forms of life they call "the higher." Those who hold the first opinion seem to mean not only that *life* and *mind* have the same denotation, but also that there is no difference in the connotation of the two terms. If so, the fathers who invented our categories for us were for once lavish in giving us two names for the same thing, whereas it was their niggardly custom to make out with one word for ten thousand things. On the other hand, those who attribute mind to the higher forms of life and not the lower escape the danger of voiding the distinction between life and mind only to fall into another more serious. For I know of none of them whose test of the presence of mind remains clear without becoming structural. But if there is anything in the poet's saying that tired limbs were invented before feather-beds and that thirst is older than wroughten cups, it may be our fathers knew a great deal about minds before they knew anything of delicate anatomy.

There is a way, however, of doing justice to both of these historic motives: the denotation of mind may be the same as that of life, and yet the connotation remain quite different. For if life were all of a level, if all things pursued the same end with no difference of skill, I cannot see how we should ever have come by the concept of mind or in what way it would have served us if we had. But in our world there are purposeful beings that differ in their aims and there are beings pursuing the same end that differ in the skill with which they make for it. Take just the latter of these classes (for I must postpone the discussion of the former to another occasion): there is no mistaking the need the biologists have felt, to account for the different resourcefulness of beings struggling for the common end of self-preservation, by introducing the category of mind. Is it not because this being has a mind the other lacks that it can adapt itself and live where the other must fail and die?

It is the observation of a certain difference of lives that has stung the primitive biologist into inventing mind. But, alas, if we ask his modern representative for a definition of this new aspect of life he either falls into mysticism or returns an answer that amounts to saying: Mind is that to have which is to have what accounts for a greater resourcefulness of behavior. Having arrived so far, he feels that any further pursuit of a problem so lacking in empirical suggestiveness is beneath his

ON SENSIBILITY

dignity as a scientist and he is ready to turn the whole matter over to a certain entity he calls the "metaphysician."

But what if, having learned a lesson from history, we were to reverse all this; what if instead of saying, "this being is more resourceful than that because it has a mind the other lacks," we were to say, "this being has a mind the other lacks because it is more resourceful?" Then all we should mean by the various faculties and graded refinements of mind would be the empirical description and measure of these differences in the conduct of life. To be sure, this would mean that if there were no comparison of minds there would be no mind at all; that we should have no reason for attributing mind to anything if we did not give it more or less than some other. But though it would be absurd to say the like of one's keys or purse or medulla, there are many concepts beside that of mind that owe their meaning to relations. Thus many of us after reading Berkeley are content to say that nothing would have any reality at all had it not more or less than some other, and would feel that he had by honest effort struggled out of the metaphysical mood that would express reality in terms of a Lockian substance whose only definition was, to be that which makes things real.[1]

[1] *Cf.* pp. 280-282.

ON SENSIBILITY

To come, then, to a definition (or rather partial definition) of mind. If one being can accomplish a given purpose in $(n+1)$ types of situation, another in but n of these, we shall call that in which the first is better equipped than the second a faculty of mind. I call this definition partial because (1) it makes comparison of means only, not of ends, and (2) it presupposes two minds, the observing and the observed whose relationship is not explained.[1] But I foresee nothing in the later discussion of these matters likely to contradict what has so far been said, although if I knew how to say everything at once I should probably want to put each thing a little differently. Lacking this gift, I do not see how any scientific discussion can avoid a certain "dialectic" that asserts only to take back in part.

Intensity of Sensation Defined

If I turn back to very ancient history to illustrate the idea set forth, I fall first upon Aristotle's distinction between animals and vegetables. With Aristotle organisms were generically alike in purpose and specifically different in resource. The first gain of resourcefulness he noted he set down to the faculties of sensibility and spontaneous motion that raised the animal above the vegetable spe-

[1] *Cf.* p. 137 sqq., "Man and Fellow-Man."

cies in the scale of life. Our modern love of continuity does not encourage us to look upon the acquisition of faculties as so sudden an affair, but we do still regard differences in the delicacy and variety of sensibility as important to the accomplishment of purpose and as evidence of mental superiority. So too spontaneity, originality, inventiveness are made measures of intelligence and are taken to be faculties that make for success. This pair, sensibility and spontaneity, might profitably be driven abreast, for I doubt if we find either of them very far apart from the other; but as I must limit myself to one (not to lengthen the discussion) I choose sensibility. Nor do I conceive that I am proposing any different problem if I offer to discuss what it means to have a sensation of a certain quality and a certain intensity.

When the sun rose on Austerlitz, it warmed a puddle and set up chemical reactions in its shallow depths; infusoria stirred; an emperor made a gesture. Inanimate matter "reacted" physically and chemically; animalcules after the manner of their various tropisms; the emperor in the fashion of a Napoleon. Why do we say that of these various reactions, that of the inanimate stuff shows something less than sensibility; that of the Emperor waving on his armies very much more; while just the simplest life there was there shows pure sensibility, nothing more and nothing less?

The answers may well lead up to a definition of sensibility. And I should say: (1) We do not call the physical and chemical reactions sensitive because they are not teleological. (2) We do not call the Emperor's gesture mere sensibility because, though full of purpose, its stimulus was not the sun's light or heat, but the sun and a fair share of the universe. (3) But we do call the behavior of the simple organism a display of sensibility because viewed as a reaction, it was teleological; and considered as to its stimulus, this stimulus was confined to mechanical changes at and within the surface of its body. Of which last the proof is, that if we imagined all the rest of the cosmos changed, but in such wise as to leave the mechanical situation at the organisms's surface unchanged, we should expect the organism to behave in the same way. It has a sensation, not a perception.

Whence this definition of sensibility: Any body that reacts with a purpose we call its own to a change of mechanical conditions within its contours displays sensibility, or has a sensation.

It follows from this that all living beings are sensitive or have sensations, but it follows equally from what went before that we should have no reason for saying so did not different living beings

ON SENSIBILITY

display such differences of sensibility as lead us to recognize sensations of varying quality and of distinguishable intensity. Wherefore it is to the definition of quality and intensity of sensation that our argument would carry us on.

The older empiricism of a Locke or of a Condillac did everything it could to foster the idea that experience began with sensations. And so it does, very possibly; but it takes a most experienced person to tell what is meant by the "simple idea" with which experience begins. What is the quality, what is the intensity of this first sensation? The learning of the ages is little enough of an equipment for the telling. It is only one who knows a great deal about the world "made out of" sensations that knows anything about the "sensations" this world is made out of. Wherefore one cannot avoid, nor should any one want to avoid, bringing as much as he can of his knowledge of mathematics and physics to bear on the task of telling what it is that a human baby or maybe a well-grown amœba has when it is said to have a sensation of this or that quality and of greater or less intensity.

To begin with intensity: only one who has developed the concept of intensity in the physical order can tell what it means in the psychical. Now to explain why, if I increase the amplitude of a light wave, I add to its intensity; while, if I alter its wave-length, I change its quality, is a matter calling for some consideration. The old opposition between quality and quantity can have no application to a state of affairs in which every term is quantitative. Why does the amplitude series constitute a scale of intensities, differences of wavelength a spectrum of qualities?

If I am not mistaken, the best English into which we can render the Latin *quale* is not *what*, but *what not!* It would seem that we endeavor to throw what differences we can into various scales of intensity; and what we cannot we leave qualitative, *i. e., not* intensive. Now a scale of intensities has this that is peculiar to it; its different members are distinguished in terms of energy. But where energy differences are not apparent in a physical series, we allow it to remain a scale of qualities. In this way we can understand how it is that two light waves of different amplitude, but constant wavelength, should be regarded as of different intensity; while two light waves of different period, but the same amplitude, should be called qualitatively different.

Having thus defined intensity of stimulus, we are free to inquire what it is in an organism's reaction to stimuli of varying intensity, or to stimuli of the same intensity under varying conditions of sensibility, that leads us to attribute to this organism sensations of different intensity.

The classic model of such an inquiry is Fechner's, the outcome of which was to define the intensity of sensation produced in a given organism by a stimulus of a given intensity in terms of the following empirical data: (1) The intensity of the physical stimulus, measured in a certain physical scale; (2) the intensity of the stimulus just noticeably greater than this; (3) the intensity of the stimulus just noticeable by the organism under the same conditions of sensibility. This definition of Fechner's meets, I conceive, all the formal demands that the traditional meaning of the term "intensity of sensation" imposes, and we need have undertaken no further labors in this field were it not for one unfortunate thing. And that is, that the third of our empirical data cannot in general be obtained. It could only be obtained for all possible cases if Weber's law could be established for all ratios of the j. n. g. stimulus to the standard, from the lower threshold stimulus to the upper. This is apparently more than can be done by experimental means so far devised; whereupon one may sum up by saying, Fechner has defined something that if it existed would be a sensation of measurable intensity; but no such thing exists.

Thus the empirical method requires us to undertake anew a reduction of vague traditional ideas respecting intensity of sensation to an exact definition that will satisfy them as well as Fechner's did, and at the same time, by avoiding all reference to Weber's law, permit us to find in experience objects corresponding to the thing we have defined. This I have tried to do with results I should like to submit to your judgment; I found the task difficult indeed, but so fascinating that it is only by the exercise of a self-restraint I hope will be counted unto me for righteousness that I abstain from plunging into a full discussion of the way this defining formula was arrived at. However, I have never found philosophers in general to share my fondness for getting my thoughts as quickly as possible into mathematical form and keeping them there as long as they would let me. Therefore, I have contented myself with submitting along with this paper the discussion referred to in case any would do me the favor to look at it: it will be enough for the present purpose if I set down the formula quite baldly:

$$I_r = a \log \frac{r - r_0}{r_\omega - r_0}.$$

That is, the intensity of the sensation due to a stimulus r is a function of exactly the same form as Fechner's and would be identical with his, if r_0 were the zero of the physical scale with respect to which Weber's law was supposed to hold and r_ω were the "threshold stimulus." I have tried to show that any definition of intensity of sensation must have this form; but that we may find a new interpretation for r_ω and r_0 that (1) makes no reference to Weber's law, (2) is indefinitely more liable to be found applicable to experience, and (3) enables us to determine the value of I_r by observing the reactions of the organism to variations of the stimulus through an indefinitely small range of values.

The data that must be collected experimentally in order that the intensity of a given sensation may be calculated can be illustrated in a particularly simple case. Jennings[1] has described the behavior of the paramecium under the influence of temperature stimuli. Placed in a trough of water kept at a temperature within a certain range, the paramecia will be found evenly distributed throughout the trough. But if one end of the trough be heated and the other cooled beyond the limits of this range, the paramecia will be found gradually to collect in the region of optimum temperature. This phenomenon comes as near as can be to an exhibition of pure sensibility; in the change of temperature of the medium we have a stimulus describable in

[1] *Amer. Jour. Phys.*, Vol. II., 1902, p. 334.

terms of mechanism; in the motion of the organism, a reaction obviously teleological; and finally, in explaining this reaction we need take into account nothing in the way of stimulus but what happens at the surface of the organism itself.

It is possible then to ask, what is the intensity of the sensation produced in a paramecium by a temperature lying within a certain range? And to this question it is incumbent on us to find an experimental answer. But this is exactly what our definition of intensity enables us to do very simply. For, suppose the organisms evenly distributed at a given temperature; suppose, then, the temperature increased at one end of the trough until the tendency is noticed for motion to take on a common direction, when we may say the organism has "just noticed" the change in its environment. The other data required for our calculation would be gathered by again decreasing the temperature until the original distribution is recovered: at a temperature which, if our formula is applicable, will not be identical with that from which we set out; but which we may define as producing a sensation of the *same intensity* under conditions of "over-estimation." Again increasing the temperature under these new conditions until the change is "just noticed," we have one group of data; and repeating the whole experiment for a range of temperatures as narrow as we please, we have all the data required for our calculation. Our definition still stands a chance of proving inapplicable, though faint indeed as compared with Fechner's. Should it prove inapplicable we should have to find new interpretations for some of the r's of our formula; but if my analysis is correct, we should be confined to a definition of the same form.

"Virtual" Behavior

I have chosen this very simple example of what an empiricist would mean by attributing a sensation of a certain intensity to a given living being, because the behavior on which the attribution rests is here so obvious. But the case is not so simple as to be free from all suggestion of difficulty. Indeed it can be made to yield one question that seems to me of great importance in defining the sort of behavior on which an empiricist bases his judgment that he is dealing with a phenomenon of mind.

"For suppose," a critic may well ask,—"suppose you had not carried out the series of experiments on which you based your calculation of the paramecium's sensation; suppose you had not varied the temperature of the medium: then there would have been no behavior on the part of the paramecium for you to observe. Would the organism have been without a sensation of a certain intensity just because you had taken no measures to ascertain what it was? On the other hand if you say it had the sensation when it did not exhibit the behavior, how can you identify sensation with behavior?"

Here, if I am not mistaken, we come upon the reason for regarding sensibility as "passive," having a sensation as a receiving rather than a doing of aught in the world. For the behavior, I would answer, that measures the intensity of our organism's sensation is not necessarily *its* behavior at all, but the behavior of certain classes of beings to which it belongs.

I have already suggested that all studies of teleologically defined being are statistical.[1] It will surprise no one then if I maintain that the order of facts on which depends my calculus of a paramecium's mental condition is quite analogous to that on which I base my estimate of a man's chance of life at a given moment. This chance of life is just as much the man's private possession as is his purse or his keys or his medulla; but whereas I can determine these latter properties without placing him in various classes to be studied by the method of averages, I can not mean anything by his chance of life save such a calculus of probabilities as actuarial experience justifies. Just so, the greater part of the "behavior" referred to by the empiricists who would define mind in terms of it, is not *actual* be-

[1] Pp. 64-69; *cf.*, p. 262 sq.

havior on the part of the being to whom this mind belongs, but *virtual* behavior; which means no more than that it is the behavior we should have reason to expect if such and such experiments were tried. But what I have called our reason to expect certain reactions can be but the experience of what actually has happened in other cases: it is a calculus of probabilities based on statistics, and may be made as accurate a calculus based on as rich a collection of statistics as our practical interest in the case justifies. Nothing but an old confusion of categories can make it seem odd that while it is A's mind we are speaking of, it is not by examining A alone, but by studying B, C, and D, that the answer to our question about A can be obtained—and that not an approximate or makeshift answer, but the only kind of answer that makes this kind of question meaningful.

Quality of Sensation Defined

While I do not propose to let myself off with a discussion of sensibility in its simplest forms only, perhaps it will be better to say what little it is necessary to say respecting the *quality* of sensation before departing from the domain of the simple. Still clinging, then, to my paramecium, it will be observed that while I was willing to discuss the intensity of its sensation due to a temperature stimulus I was careful to avoid speaking of this as a sensation of heat. For imagine an organism so simply constituted that although it reacts to stimuli of different quality (light, heat, chemical, electrical) it responds to all of them in the same way. Let us suppose its only way of reacting to any stimulus is to move, would there be any reason for attributing to it different qualities of sensation because it moved in response to different qualities of stimulus? If we had to find a name for the quality of its sensation, would it not be enough to call it a sensation of discomfort; whether light, heat, chemical changes, electricity, or whatever else was responsible for its state?

It is only, then, when a subject responds to one quality of stimulus in a way it does not react to another that we have reason for attributing to it sensations of different quality. As the development of reactions specific to different qualities of stimulus goes hand in hand with the development of specific sense-organs, we are only too likely to fall back on a structural definition of the qualitative differences of sensation: "The sensation that results from stimulating the eye has the quality of color, while what comes from stimulating the ear has the quality of sound." *A la bonne heure;* but a man who reacts in the same way to a stimulus of red and to one of green is easily recognized to be color-blind long before we know anything about the structural defect in his retina that goes with this infirmity. In short, it is the difference in reaction to different qualities of stimulus that defines qualitative differences of sensation: what relation this difference bears to structure is a secondary question.

Finally, it is evident from our definition of quality as the *what not*, increase in the variety and richness of experience is constantly changing the meaning of *each* quality as it is differentiated from more and more *others*. Whence nothing could be more misleading than the account our older empiricism offers of the way in which experience, beginning with simple ideas (or as Helmholtz called them *qualia*), leaves these unmodified and only learns to recognize new combinations of them. It can be no truer that I begin with *qualia* and come by a knowledge of the world, than that I begin with a world and come by a knowledge of the *qualia*.

The Higher Forms of Sensibility

I have, I see, allowed myself but scant space in which to discuss the phenomena of sensibility in the higher forms of life; but fortunately little more is needed than to adapt the principles already laid down to somewhat changed conditions. As long as I confined myself to those very simple forms of life, the exciting cause of whose behavior lay in their immediate surroundings and was susceptible of a purely mechanical description, it was not hard to tell what behavior I meant when I defined their mental life in terms of their actual and virtual behavior. But as we ascend in the scale of life the stimulus to actual behavior becomes more and more complex and more and more of the mechanical conditions at the surface of the subject's body may change without altering the trend of his present conduct; while a larger and larger share of the universe remote from the subject can not be conceived different and his conduct remain the same. Thus as I sit writing, the blue of the sky out of the window, the crackling of the logs on the hearth, are of so little importance to what I have on hand that the sky might lose much of its light and the fire die down to silence and yet no change in my behavior be noted. Yet it is not denied that I do receive sensations of some sort from these and a thousand other things in and around me, so that the impression is deepened that to have a sensation is a very passive sort of experience.

Nor, being rather a lover of old terms than an innovator, do I see why sensations should not even from the point of view of the kind of empiricism I have been arguing for continue to be spoken of as passively received impressions of a certain quality and of a certain intensity. But I should interpret this to mean that the behavior one appeals to define mind in its various aspects must of course include the behavior that doesn't take place as well as the behavior that does. What indeed is meant by asserting that the sky's blue is less intense and qualitatively vaguer to me than to my artist neighbor who is trying to paint it? Is it not that a change in this intensity or in this quality which would make him reach for a new color would leave me scribbling with the same pen? But some degrees of change would disturb me too: if there were no way of estimating this virtual behavior of mine (as there would be none if I were blind) I should not be credited with a sensation of light. After all, sensibility in man is very much like sensibility in the paramecium and I hardly regret that I have left myself so little space in which to deal with it.

The Inner Mental Life

Having come so far on the way to a definition of sensation, its quality and intensity, I was sensible the way had been dry; and if I was not to overtax the patience of even such tried travelers as those who had invited me to lead them for once, it was time I hastened on to some sort of a stopping place. Therefore with a brief reference to the sensory material of dream-life, I left my argument to the judgment of those for whom half a word is more than enough. But as it has seemed to very distinguished writers (such as Henri Bergson) that the recognition of sensation as existing where neither stimulus nor reaction is observable to the onlooker was an altogether convincing argument against going to work on the definition of sensation in the way I have, it will be wiser to take a more leisurely survey of this field and to devote a separate article to a consideration of the inner mental life.[1]

[1] *Vid.* p. 109 sqq., "On Pain and Dreams."

DISCUSSION OF SENSATION-INTENSITY

VI.

DISCUSSION OF SENSATION-INTENSITY

If r is a stimulus measured in some physical scale of intensity, and if $f(r_1, r_2)$ is the difference of sensation-intensity produced by the stimuli r_1 and r_2, respectively, then

Post. 1.—$f(r_1, r_2) + f(r_2, r_3) = f(r_1, r_3)$

which has for its solution

$$f(r_1, r_2) = \phi(r_1) - \phi(r_2).$$

If $\phi(r)$ is to have the properties traditionally given to the intensity of a sensation produced by the stimulus r, then

Post. 2.—The intensity of the sensation produced by stimulus r is independent of the *zero* of the physical scale in which r is measured.

Wherefore all r-dimensioned quantities must appear in pairs of the form

$$(r_\alpha - r_\beta).$$

Post. 3.—The intensity of the sensation produced by stimulus r is independent of the *unit* of the physical scale in which r is measured.

DISCUSSION OF SENSATION-INTENSITY

Wherefore all r-dimensioned quantities must appear in quadrads of the form
$$\left(\frac{r_\alpha - r_\beta}{r_\gamma - r_\delta}\right).$$

To interpret r_α, r_β, etc., empirically, let the place of r_α be taken by the stimuli r_1, r_2, etc., and let r_{1+}, r_{2+}, *etc.*, be their just noticeably greater stimuli. Let $r_\beta = r_\delta = r_0$, in which r_0 is some degree of the physical scale in which r is measured, such that the equation holds

$$\frac{r_{1+} - r_0}{r_1 - r_0} = \frac{r_{2+} - r_0}{r_2 - r_0},$$

or, solving,
$$r_0 = \frac{r_1 r_{2+} - r_{1+} r_2}{r_1 + r_{2+} - r_{1+} - r_2}.$$

If Weber's law held and if we imagined r_1 to remain constant while r_2 varied, r_0 would have a constant value.

But it is less of an assumption to suppose, not that r_0 remains constant under these conditions, but that it approaches a limit as r_2 approaches r_1. In place of Weber's zero we take, then,

Post. 4.—
$$r_0 = \lim_{r_2 \doteq r_1} \left(\frac{r_1 r_{2+} - r_{1+} r_2}{r_1 + r_{2+} - r_{1+} - r_2}\right),$$

and substituting the r's so far defined, we have

$$\varphi(r) = \varphi\left(\frac{r-r_0}{r_\gamma - r_0}\right).$$

Interpreting r_γ to be the intensity of the stimulus that produces a sensation of zero intensity and writing $r_\gamma = r_\omega$, we may define r_ω by

Post. 5.—

$$\varphi\left(\frac{r_\omega - r_0}{r_\omega - r_0}\right) = 0,$$

and substituting r_ω for r_γ, we have

$$\varphi(r) = \varphi\left(\frac{r-r_0}{r_\omega - r_0}\right).$$

Post. 6.—Subjective conditions remaining constant, the intensity of the sensation produced by a changing stimulus is a continuous function of that stimulus.

Therefore, since our data is experimental, with a probable error attached, we may always find lying within the limits of p. e. an analytic function of r that will satisfy the conditions imposed upon $\phi(r)$.

Post. 7.—Subjective conditions remaining constant, the *rate* at which the intensity of sensation varies with the stimulus is independent of what we take to be the sensation of zero intensity.

DISCUSSION OF SENSATION-INTENSITY

Since r_ω is defined as the stimulus producing a sensation of zero intensity, this amounts to saying

$$\frac{\partial}{\partial r_\omega}\left(\frac{\partial}{\partial r}\varphi\left(\frac{r-r_0}{r_\omega-r_0}\right)\right) = 0.$$

Post. 8.—Subjective conditions remaining constant, the intensity of sensation increases with the stimulus.

From the postulates so far laid down, we have for the form of $\phi(r)$

$$\varphi(r) = a \log \frac{r-r_0}{r_\omega-r_0}.$$

a being a constant essentially positive.

But our formula has as yet failed to make explicit those "subjective conditions" of sensibility that have been traditionally accepted as playing a part in the intensity of sensation produced by a given stimulus. As these have been made to depend on the j. n. g. stimulus r_+, we must determine how this r_+ enters into our expression. To do this consider the case in which a unit difference of intensity exists between $\phi(r_2)$ and $\phi(r_1)$, $(r_2 > r_1)$, subjective conditions remaining constant. That is,

$$a \log \frac{r_2-r_0}{r_\omega-r_0} - a \log \frac{r_1-r_0}{r_\omega-r_0} = 1,$$

or, solving,

$$a = \frac{1}{\log \dfrac{r_2 - r_0}{r_1 - r_0}}.$$

Here the only arbitrary quantity is r_2, so that if the j. n. g. stimulus is to appear in our formula at all it must be included in our definition of r_2. Whence

Post. 9.—$r_2 = f(r_{1+})$.

But since from Post. 2 the r's of our formula can enter only in the form $(r_\alpha - r_\beta)$, it follows that

$$f(r_{1+}) = r_{1+}$$

and if we now designate by the symbol $I(r_1)$, the intensity of the sensation produced by stimulus r, we have for a given stimulus r_1

$$I(r_1) = \frac{1}{\log \dfrac{r_{1+} - r_0}{r_1 - r_0}} \cdot \log \frac{r_1 - r_0}{r_\omega - r_0}$$

There only remains to be selected the empirical meaning of r_ω. Fechner took r_ω to be the threshold-stimulus and so made the applicability of his definition to hang on the truth of Weber's law. A phenomenon much better established by experience is that of the over-estimation of the second stimulus. Let r' be the stimulus that under conditions of over-estimation is judged equal to r; r_+' the stimulus that under the same conditions is just noticeably greater than r', and r_0' the analogue of r_0. We shall define a particular case of zero difference of intensity by

Post. 10.— $\qquad I(r) - I(r') = 0.$

We may now solve this equation for r_ω. The solution is particularly simple when $r_0' = r_0$, and as these may be anticipated to be very close-lying quantities, we might for practical purposes identfy them with r_0.

Writing for brevity

$$\frac{r_+ - r_0}{r - r_0} = k$$

we readily obtain the final numerical value

$$I(r_1) = \left(\log \frac{k}{k'} \right)^{-1} \cdot \log \frac{r_1 - r_0}{r_1' - r_0}.$$

The empirical question of the truth of Weber's law depends upon our ability to find conditions under which the subjective parameters k, k'_0, r_0 remain constant. This is only a special case of the more general experimental problem, How do these parameters vary with the conditions of the experiment in which r is made to vary?

ON PAIN AND DREAMS

VII.

ON PAIN AND DREAMS

Retrospect

In my last article contributed to this Journal,[1] I began by offering some very general reflections on the meaning of mind, and followed these with a rather minute study of one of the most anciently and broadly recognized faculties of mind, sensibility. These reflections presupposed that one would not attempt a definition of mind without first having constructed an image of nature as a mechanism, and then drawn such a picture of life making its way through this mechanism as would leave to living beings all that purposive freedom which seems to be their defining trait. In this way at any rate my own thought had proceeded, first imagining the whole spread of nature to be at all points a mechanism, then following through this mechanism the progress of certain groups of these same points. The passage of each such group was in some ways that of a slow-moving pulse, losing and gaining

[1] This article, prepared in fulfilment of the closing promise of V, was not brought to prompt completion. The first sections stand in their original wording. The section on "Dreams" is added.

constituents as it went, yet never leaving its own identity in doubt nor ever violating the laws of the medium through which its course lay. In other ways this passing form was more like those little whirlwinds we see hurrying down the street, setting things aside for their passage, yet never ceasing to be of the same stuff and law as the other air through which they move.

But what is peculiar to the class of groups we have now before us is this: if an observer were to follow the histories of the groups of this class, he would find them on the whole to result in a common type of phenomenon. We should consider him to be recording this observation in the most suitable form were he to announce: the beings of this class have only the purpose of their behavior in common. For I had indeed meant to select from all the dissimilar pulses moving through the medium of nature's mechanism a class of pulses defined only by similarity of purpose. And when finally from all the classes susceptible of being thus (teleologically) defined I had selected that one whose typical purpose was "self-preservation," I expected the members of this class to be recognized by all as the bodies of living beings.

So it was that before approaching the problem of mind, I had tried to think of life as a pulse or vortex, partly propagated, partly spending its energy to force its way through a uniform sea of mechanism whose laws remain unbroken by the purposive gestures of these animate portions of itself. Nor did any fear of contradiction deter me from defining as purposeful and recognizing as free the organism whose only stuff and material was that of the medium in which it moved and of which it was. For the categories of mechanism apply only to the point, those of teleology only to the group of points; and what logician would hesitate to assign to a number of things taken collectively, properties he may previously have denied to these same things taken distributively? From only two historic suggestions do our assumptions exclude us: (1) the materialism that struggles to define the living whole in the terms it has used for the mechanical parts, (2) the monadism that feels called upon to define the mechanical parts in terms it has employed on the living whole. But what promise of continuity these classic suggestions seem in their opposite ways to hold out to us, we cheerfully forego; confident that logic is better served by insisting upon rather than deprecating the discontinuity that breaks any transition from a distributive to a collective *all*.

Coming thus to the threshold of *mind*, seeking the historic motives that have forced man's descriptive effort to add the category of mind to that of life, we found in our world but one thing that might be absent though life were present. And that thing is *difference of life;* mind is called upon to explain why one living being is "higher," another "lower." "Higher"? That is to say, able to attain its goal in a wider range of circumstances; and so "freer," whether with a freedom enhanced by resource in means, or with an emancipation won by choice of end. With this understanding of life's differences, would it seem too much for an empiricist to assume that if mind was traditionally what made for success, then some of what made for success was mind?

In two ways, we say, history has invoked mind to account for elevation or emancipation of life. To superiority of mind has been attributed that resource or skill which enables one life to win what another must lose. And to superiority of mind again has been laid that wisdom or reasonableness in the choice of ideals which in all times has been taken to distinguish the philosopher from the man of no thought. As no one looking for the simplest beginning would turn to the "rationality" displayed in ideals for a first hint as to the meaning of mind, the article we are here recalling confined itself to the mentality exhibited in resource or skill. Thus restricting ourselves to a comparison of lives in terms of their resource, we considered that resource in attaining an end prescribed could most demonstrably be measured in terms of the range of circumstances

ON PAIN AND DREAMS

in which the subject is well-calculated to win out. Tersely, we ventured to put the first part of a definition of mind into a formula:

If one living being can accomplish a given purpose in $(n+1)$ types of situation, another in but n of these, we call that (non-mechanical) quality in which the first is better equipped than the second *a faculty of mind.*

Whereupon, passing from general considerations to a particular study of that faculty of mind we call sensibility, I could find no more promising clue to what we might mean by this, than such as was suggested by an unavoidably technical discussion of *intensity of sensation.* (As for the qualitative difference of sensations, I was content to let that go for any sort of difference *not* intensive). For one holding firmly to the empirical method, the model for a discussion of intensity is set by the psychophysical study of reaction to variations of stimulus; and of all such studies, those of Fechner, based on the observations of Weber, command the first attention. Weber had recorded certain empirical results; Fechner, whatever he may have thought himself to be doing, used the suggestion of these results to formulate a psychophysical definition of intensity of sensation.

It must lie close to any philosopher's heart to analyze out of Fechner's definition (regarding his so-called *law* as pure definition) those things anyone would see in "intensity of sensation," and to distinguish them from those other things that only one who assumed the empirical soundness of Weber's law would venture to put there.

The results of such an inquiry constitute the pith of the article to which this is a sequel, and it is necessary for my present purpose to recall no more of them than this much: If imposing upon our definition only such conditions as the plainest of men would admit to be part of the common notion of intensity of sensation we seek the formula having just these implications, we come out with an expression like Fechner's in form, differing only in the number of parameters and in the empirical interpretation of some of them. This is an important difference indeed, from the point of view of the applicability of the concept defined; but it changes nothing of the methodological idea. We are but following a classic suggestion in holding sensation, its intensity, and what as *not* its intensity we call its quality, to be completely definable in terms of observed or calculable reactions to observed or observable physical stimuli. For the way in which the definition may be relieved of dependence on Weber's law, I must refer to the original article. I was there content to define intensity of sensation as a certain mathematical function of such quantities as Fechner used, (1) the stimulus, (2) a "just noticeably" different stimulus; but avoided identifying any of our parameters with what would be empirically meaningful only if Weber's law held true for finite differences of stimulus.

IMMEDIACY AND REFLECTION

We may repeat however that nothing in this departure from technical tradition affects the classic thesis. Empirical psychology has long had at its disposal a means of treating sensation in general, its intensity in particular, as an object of accurate observation. For this reason we have been able to use the actual procedure of the psychophysicist to illustrate the observation of mental states. We have but developed for a particularly difficult case our first principle of empirical method: The key to the definition of whatever thing, is to be found in the practice of the science looking for that sort of thing. And we might add this corollary: No definition is meaningful which pretends to stand for something no experimental practice can find, or at least measure its approach to.

To the general objections that would spring from the classic empiricism of the eighteenth century, our account of a more thorough-going empirical method has given ample consideration in earlier pages: it was of course impossible for a philosophy attempting to construct a world out of immediately given sensations to recognize sensations as remote objects of search for men of this world. But *specific* criticism of our definitions could not be forthcoming from a school of thought to which the like of our procedure had neither suggested itself nor been suggested. Such definite argument had to wait for our own more experienced day, whose wits had sharpened themselves on the long struggle of the psychophysicists to interpret their experimental material. It is to a Bergson I would turn for the most lucid expression of an order of objection likely to have presented itself to the mind of many a reader as our exposition progressed.

Of this problem of intensity, we find Bergson writing: "The solution which occurs immediately to the mind . . . consists in defining the intensity of a sensation, or of any state whatever of the ego, by the number and magnitude of the objective, and therefore measurable, causes which have given rise to it. Doubtless a more intense sensation of light is one which has been obtained, or is obtainable, by means of a larger number of luminous sources, provided they be at the same distance and identical with one another. But, in the immense majority of cases, we decide about the intensity of the effect without even knowing the nature of the cause, much less its magnitude: indeed, it is the very intensity of the effect which often leads us to venture an hypothesis as to the number and nature of the causes, and thus to revise the judgment of our senses, which at first represented them as insignificant. And it is no use arguing that we are then comparing the actual state of the ego with some previous state in which the cause was perceived in its entirety at the same time as its effect was experienced. No doubt this is our procedure in a fairly large number of cases; but we cannot then explain the differences of intensity which we recognize between deep-seated psychic phenomena, the cause of which is within us and not outside. On the other hand, we are never so bold in judging the intensity of a psychic state as when the subjective aspect of the phenomena is the only one to strike us, or when the external cause to which we refer it does not easily admit of measurement. Thus it seems evident that we experience a more intense pain at the pulling out of a tooth than of a hair; the artist knows without the possibility of doubt that the picture of a master affords him more intense pleasure than the signboard of a shop; and there is not the slightest need ever to have heard of forces of cohesion to assert that we expend less effort in bending a steel blade than a bar of iron. Thus the comparison of two intensities is usually made without the least appreciation of the number of causes, their mode of action, or their extent."[1]

I have reproduced this passage at length, because it sets forth so clearly all that other and older empiricisms must hold against our more radical extension of the empirical method. Some of the motives of its antagonism are still quite general; for a Bergson as for a Locke the objective world is built of "immediate data of consciousness," and it is natural to expect qualitative differences of sensation to furnish the most immediate of this data. It is then Bergson's cue to interpret intensive differences as special arrangements of qualitative differences of sensation. In all this, the newer empiricism shares the motives of the older which we have so frequently examined and refused. There are however certain parts of Bergson's criticism that would seem forcible enough to arrest even one who up to this point had accepted our ideal of empirical procedure. They baffle him by pointing to familiar instances in which objective data for a calculation of intensity cannot be obtained, and yet in which the subjective judgment of intensity spontaneously wells up: they adduce those "deep-seated psychic phenomena, the cause of which is within us and not outside."

[1] *Time and Free Will*, pp. 4-6.

Pain

Here indeed, it may plausibly be maintained, "the subjective aspect of the phenomenon is the only one to strike us [since] the external cause to which we refer it does not easily admit of measurement." Now as our whole plan has been to put the meaning of intensity into an inference from stimuli-differences observed to have been noticed, to differences calculated to be noticeable, how are we to envisage a situation like this? An essential part of the data from which calculation is to proceed is lacking; and not to the subject only, but to the most reflective observer as well. Yet neither is at a loss to recognize differences in intensity of sensation! Could one require of the most sophisticated reflection that it recognize a triangle from an exposure of but two of its sides?

To a question so embarrassing to our own empiricism, Bergson's offers a ready answer:

"The intensity of affective sensations [pleasure, pain] might . . . be nothing more than our consciousness of the involuntary movements which are being begun and outlined, so to speak, within these states, and which would have gone on their own way if nature had made us automata instead of conscious beings.

"If such be the case, we shall not compare a pain

ON PAIN AND DREAMS

of increasing intensity to a note which grows louder and louder, but rather to a symphony, in which an increasing number of instruments make themselves heard. Within the characteristic sensation, which gives the tone to all the others, consciousness distinguishes a larger or smaller number of sensations arising at different points of the periphery, muscular contractions, organic movements of every kind: the choir of these elementary psychic states voices the new demands of the organism, when confronted by a new situation. In other words, we estimate the intensity of a pain by the larger or smaller part of the organism which takes interest in it."[1]

The trouble with this explanation is not that it misrepresents facts, but simply that it does not explain. It does not explain why in one case "the larger or smaller part of the organism which takes interest in it" is a measure of a sensation's intensity, while in plenty of other cases a spreading or narrowing of the parts of us taking interest in some particular experience measures no such thing. A rose grows none the sweeter to the nostril for having won the eye as well. Here is indeed an expansion in the part of the organism which takes interest in the rose; but it is *the wrong kind of expansion*. One sector of my book-shelves is not less intense than two because one makes demand on my eye

[1] *Op. cit.*, p. 34.

alone while two must invoke the interest of my neck as well. Less of me is involved in the first exploitation; but *not the right less.*

No doubt, after we have come by the concept of the intensity of pain, we can use that complexity of reaction which we now know to be the right kind of complexity, to guess at the increasing energy of some unknown stimulus. One term of the stimulus-reaction relation is enough, *now*, for at least a rough estimate of intensity; but could it have been enough from the first?

What would seem to be a real alternative to the interpretation of these intensity-judgments as exclusively "subjective," is the suggestion that would have them to be inspired by an instinctive use of analogy. Nor does such an hypothesis call for any but the most elementary processes of reasoning on the part of the acquiring subject. He sees, let us suppose, the grimace and contortions of a man suffering (as the physician will presently inform him) from an intensifying colic; he can of course make no observation or measurement of that increasing gas-pressure which is a stimulus, as Bergson has it, "inside of us and not outside." Yet as the simplest observer who has ever witnessed the reaction called forth by increasing *external* pressure, watches the patient pass from a faint frown, through all the familiar phases of bodily contortion, to a paroxysmal stiffening of the whole frame, is it likely he would here fail to sense "increasing intensity of pain"? On the other hand, had we never taken mutely spreading reactions to *observable* stimuli to measure the increasing painfulness of these stimuli, where should we now find argument for interpreting similar reactions to *hidden* stimuli in this way? I can think of no *a priori* reason why one sort of spreading reaction should be interpreted as increasing intensity of sensation, another as increasing extensity of perception, a third as growing complexity of experience of any sort you please.

While then in this as in all cases of judging intensity by reaction alone, we may indeed "decide about the intensity of the effect without even knowing the nature of the cause, much less its magnitude," the way we came by this ability cannot have been other than a series of psychophysical observations on stimuli and reactions.

But such estimates of intensity are necessarily crude, and are only cited to suggest how man in the rough might have come by a rough way of estimating intensities of unknown stimulation while waiting data for finer calculation. No definition however is in the full spirit of the empirical method if it suggest no experimental way by which a question of fact may be answered within any required degree of accuracy. My ideas of mass would be in a sorry state did they let me explain no more than how by them primitive man might have known a boulder for more massive than a pebble; and my notions of intensity would be in no better way did they only justify me in concluding that pulling a tooth must hurt more than pulling a hair.

As a first step toward developing an accurate phychophysics of "deep-seated psychic phenomena," it may be recalled that the intensity of sensation in this domain has always expressed itself in a two-fold idiom. The hunger of an all-day fast is the hunger that "could eat an oxe"; the weariness of an all-night vigil is the weariness that "could sleep the clock 'round"; and the thirst of a salt diet "would drink the river dry." And so with pain; it has a natural measure in its counter-stimulus, its anodyne. I remember a physician, wishing to convey to me the agony of a certain affliction, choosing as the immediately intelligible phrase: "It is a pain no morphine can kill." The measure of these sensations in terms of their cure must be as primitive as their measure in terms of their cause; it must be as ancient as life's reaching for relief; it must be as ancient as life.

Nothing then should be more feasible than to set up experiments on pain (to speak of that) in which by varying the counter-stimulus, the anodyne; by observing the "just noticeable difference" in such stimulation; by following in general the psychophysical procedure of our previous article, we should effect as accurate a measurement of the intensity of pain as ever we did of any category of sensation.

Dreams

But doubtless the most striking difficulty facing one who would treat sensation as an observable object is presented by the phenomena of dreams. In the classic problem of psychophysics, the ease with which we could identify and measure the stimulus, the definiteness with which we could point to a significant and observable reaction ("noticing a difference") gave us every ease in presenting as an object of observation the psychic thing called a sensation. Only for a moment did the phenomena of "deep-seated psychic states" threaten our interpretation, by adducing judgments of intensity of sensation, shut-off from observation of stimulus. The difficulty proved but passing: for all purposes of observation and measurement, the unobservable direct stimulus could be replaced by an observable counter-stimulus, and the psychophysical data necessary to the recognition of intensity be collected.

When however it occurs to us that sensations may exist and be recognized under circumstances in which reflection excludes, not the accessibility merely, but the very existence of stimuli, we are tempted to abandon the cause. And for what else than sensations lacking stimuli can we take the sensory material of dreams? Is not a dream a mental state to which no object corresponds? And if this is the characteristic of the whole, must it not be that of any part? So that if to the dream-tree no objective tree corresponds, for the *green* of the dream-tree no green-stimulus can be found. In which case, from the point of view of no conceivable reflection can the intensity accorded a dream-sensation be an attribution based on a study of noticed differences in stimuli—in stimuli granted not to exist. Yet who could be so devoted to our "empirical method" as rather to deny existence to dream-sensations than admit "sensation" to be not the sort of thing we have taken it to be?

It is to be doubted however whether this naïve, this poet's conception of "a dream and an imagining" is altogether that of the modern psychologist. Is a dream indeed an imagining? That is, is it altogether an imagining? There has developed from the more recent study of dreams a tendency on the part of psychology to view at least some dreams as *occasioned* by definite physical events in a way strikingly suggestive of that in which sensations are *stimulated*.

Every one knows, and literature is full of, the sort

of dream that opportunely befell the writer in the midst of his recent preoccupation with dream-theory. Waking immediately on its culmination and having its family somewhat on his conscience, he was in position and mood to jot down certain of its peculiarities.

The plot developed and the scene shifted with the inconsequence usual to dreams, without exciting the dreamer's wonder or protest till toward the very end. An afternoon-hour in the grounds of a familiar country-place; friends discussing Kant's "moral law"; a servant interrupting to announce "one waiting on the phone," whither hastening the dreamer finds himself making for the kitchen-extension in his own city-house—some fifty miles away. Singular taste; unaccountable contempt for convenience! And yet there is this to be said for the choice: this phone is the only one of the writer's waking world, access to which could be obstructed by a carelessly-open door. Now it will immediately appear that such a door was, if not indispensable, at least highly convenient to the working out of the plot. For hastening to the phone, and finding indeed this door in his way, the hero of our dream flung it impatiently to. Followed the catastrophe! A screech, scream, shriek—how call that whose like ne'er was on sea or land? Cook (or some dim handy body) pointed to the dog's tail, caught under the door. And although even in his dream the outcry struck him as difficult to reconcile with the performance of his own or any known breed of dog, the dreamer let himself be content, in his haste to reach the phone. But the play was out; came some meaningless mumblings over the wire; the dreamer awoke. His first waking moments caught as it were an echo of that cry: he was aware of an auto-horn that distance had not yet robbed of all its unlovely quality.

Concerning the matter and occasion of his dream, the writer ventures certain speculations within the sympathy of common experience and not without the interest of psychology:

(1) Of a sufficient number of sleepers within range of such a horn-blast, more will dream within a brief interval following, than had silence prevailed. We may call the dreams in excess of the normal "occasioned dreams."

(2) Of dreams occasioned by a sound-event, a larger proportion will culminate in a sound-episode than of dreams occasioned by an inaudible event (*e. g.* mechanical shock). This excess we may call "sound-occasioned dreams."

(3) Of sound-occasioned dreams, the range of quality and intensity attributed to the sound-episode will be wider if comparison be made throughout the

whole group than if it be confined to the sub-group occasioned by a sound-event of one quality and intensity.

Recent phychology, we have noted, sees in a dream-situation of the kind described, (1) a mechanical event analogous to *stimulus*, (2) a bit of organic history analogous to *reaction*. In fact, what is here lacking of the data regarded in psychophysical experiment as sufficient warrant for attributing sensation to the subject? The stimulus? But we may surely anticipate actual experiment to the extent of assuming that if in place of the "horn-blast" the occasion of the dream had been any other happening affecting the ear with the same air-vibrations, the same reactions, *caeteris paribus*, would have followed. So far then, the *occasion* of the dream-sound fulfils the conditions we have laid upon a *sensory stimulus*.[1] And what of the reaction?

The reaction actually observed (the subject's description) is of course under no such experimental control as is the type employed in accurate psychophysical measurement. No device is within immediate prospect whereby, varying the stimulus by gradual increments (let us say), we may catch the subject "just noticing a difference." But in this very effort to measure our distance from the ideal, we only confess that ideal the more explicitly; it

[1] *Vid.* p. 84.

is the ideal of our happier psychophysical moments. The bit of organic history we are in search of is the *sensory reaction.*

It is not hard to see why the psychologist ("speaking with probability," as Plato would say) takes the dream-dog's yelp to have at its core as true a sensation as has any dog-yelp of the waking world, or as had the recognized horn-blast that assailed the dreamer's ears immediately on waking.

And now the writer would willingly go on to what he conceives should be the next step required of any method taking temporary refuge in an experimental "ideal." No ideal is one unless it can be shown to be experimentally approachable: otherwise it is an empty "unknowable." Nor do I think the experimental way so hidden as to defy indication: I should be tempted to begin by suggesting a continuity of transition from waking perception, through hallucination (in which there is something like a simultaneity of waking and dreaming) to the dream of deeper sleep and postponed awakening. Now these hallucinations furnish very approximately the conditions of ordinary psychophysical experiment, and while I have found in literature no formal attempt to measure the intensity of hallucinatory sensations, there is reported by Sokolow a close observation of "noticed" changes of pitch and rythm, with a reference to which, by way of hint, I must here content myself.[1]

But if to keep within the *cadre* I must needs leave some ways unexplored, I should not want the approach to a question raised at the outset to be one of these. My dream-story opened in the grounds of a country-place: this place in my waking world has its lawns and shade like another. So, I presume, did the place of my dreams; though my only realization was one of full familiarity. Supplying these lawns and trees, they must be painted-in green; else how could they have been "familiar"? Query: Was this *green*, too, a sensation; or only an "imagining"?

I see no reason why I, or any one, should know —as yet. But we shall have done all a theory of empirical method can be asked to do by such a problem if we reduce it to one susceptible of experimental investigation. And this much, I hope, can be done.

The story of my dream I tried to tell in such a way as to induce in the reader the mood of that more recent psychology which would interpret the whole series of my dream-episodes as an attempt on the part of a sleeper to "apperceive" an actual stimulus,

[1] *Archiv f. Psychiatrie u. Nervenkrankheiten*, 55, 432: "Die experimentelle Auslösung d. Gehörshalluzinationen durch periphere Reize." Also, *op. cit.* 56, 174: "Weitere Experimente usw."

the stimulus whose repetition was later apperceived as "receding auto-horn." Country-places, Kantian moralities, phones, dogs—all that—were dragged-in (as Lucretius anciently surmised) from the depths of my own past. But in apperceiving the repeated stimulus, too, much was dragged-in out of that past; only it was not so personal to my past: others who knew not Kant might have shared it. Now the auto to which this horn belonged was (as all the neighbors would have recognized) passing through a city park: were not the city trees as green to my waking thought as the country trees to my dreaming?

The problem we began with is not then peculiarly a dream problem; waking life too has its aura of "imaginings" with which in perception it clothes upon a stimulated core of sensation. Is this (or the part of it requiring sensory description) a "complex idea of sensation"?

And now I can perhaps put the promised suggestion as to the meaning these entirely kindred questions have for experiment in very brief form. Suppose experimental physiology to have made it probable enough to argue from, that for any one of these "imaginings" in which dreaming and perceiving alike enfold their sensory "data," there is a mechanical "occasion." Are these "occasioning" events stimuli? To my mind the question is equivalent to asking: Are these events (each mechanical enough) *mechanically alike*, or are they only *teleologically alike?* The same sort of question led us on a former occasion to reflect that time-pieces, though each a mechanism, presented a class of such disparate mechanisms as permitted no mechanical definition of the class. Just so, if the brain event without which *you* would not have imagined color, and the brain-event without which *I* should not, have no other likeness than in the *reactions* they occasion in us, then they are not *stimuli*. And if they are not stimuli, then no reaction to them is to be described as *sensation*, however sensory the descriptive terms in which on reflection it expresses itself. On the other hand there is no *a priori* reason for assuming the brain events occasioning "color-images" in divers subjects to be more various in their mechanism than the extra-corporeal events stimulating "color sensations." And should these brain-events prove to be thus mechanically alike, their place of occurrence would in no wise exclude them from the class of true stimuli: any reaction to them yielding the (teleological) phenomenon of "just-noticing," would have every claim to be called a sensation.

The issue is empirical; but the experiment we have invoked to determine it is once more "ideal." Is there no present suggestion of a way to approach this ideal? There is at least this: the study of "vicarious functioning" considers the extent to which one part of the organism can replace another in occasioning the same reaction. Is it not from such studies that we may expect some hint as to whether or not different *parts* with the same function represent different *mechanisms* with the same function? On such experimental issues our decision must turn.

But neither way of turning can take us in the direction of a "mechanistic" interpretation of sensibility.

MAN AND FELLOW-MAN

VIII.

MAN AND FELLOW-MAN [1]

At every turn of my thought respecting the meaning of truth, I am met by a figure that has no dwelling on sea or land and whom I have come to call the Man Without a Fellow. It is strange that so lonely a phantom should have anything in his aspect to trouble the quiet of a philosopher, yet the more I consider him, the more the impression forces itself on me that he holds in his hands the fate of my philosophy and of the science of many another.

I say the science of many another must be concerned for the laying of this ghost, if ghost he be, yet it is exactly because the philosophers of our own day who I should have thought had most to fear from him have either noticed him not at all or passed him cavalierly by, that I wonder whether I can have understood these philosophers aright.

Have I, for example, caught the meaning of the "instrumentalist" when he insists upon the "social reference" of even the most intimate of our personal experiences? "The fact is," writes Professor

[1] Paper read (by proxy) before the American Philosophical Association at New York, December, 1912.

Dewey, summing up the case for instrumentalism, —"the fact is that the life, the experience of the individual man, is already saturated, thoroughly interpenetrated, with social inheritances and references. . . . Education, language, and other means of communication are infinitely more important categories of knowledge than any of those exploited by absolutists. And as soon as the methodological battle of instrumentalism is won . . . the two services that will stand to the credit of instrumentalism will be calling attention first to the connection of intelligence with a genuine future, and, second, to the social constitution of personal, even of private experience, above all of any experience that has assumed the knowledge-form."

Do I, I ask, take Mr. Dewey aright in supposing him here to be not merely calling attention to certain facts respecting the psychology of a being who *happens* to stand in various social relations with others of his kind? He is rather, is he not, deducing from the very meaning of truth and error certain conditions without which truth and error, and so experience, knowledge, mind, can neither be nor be conceived? He means, does he not, that consciousness is so essentially social in its reference that if there were no society to refer to, there would be no consciousness to refer? He means, in a word, that it takes at least two minds to make one; as Fichte has put it, *"ein Mensch ist nur unter Menschen ein Mensch?"*

If this is what the instrumentalist stands for, then the image of our man without a fellow must be as critical for his philosophy as for mine, and nothing could more quickly and effectively clear the way for his onward march than the removal of this enigmatic figure from his path. But if the instrumentalist means less than this—if he means no more than to observe that minds which happen to have been brought in contact are so profoundly affected by this accident of their history that the result is better symbolized as an interpenetration than as a point or surface contact—then instrumentalism may have called attention to an interesting fact of psychology, but I fail to see in what sense the categories used to arrive at this conclusion can be judged either more or less important than "those exploited by absolutists." For the absolutist is not interested in these historical accidents of mind, not merely because he hopes in the end to show that there are no historical accidents, but also because at no stage of his reasoning does it appear to him accidental that the finite mind owes its being and its meaning to its fellowship with another mind. For him quite frankly it takes two minds to make one, and one of the two is the Absolute. Therefore

I should expect him to take up the instrumentalist's reflection on his categories in some such terms as these: I am trying, he would say, to arrive at a definition of truth; if you are only interested in some accidents that attach to truth as it is found in this or that empirical situation, we have no quarrel, for we have no common problem. If, however, you have my problem in mind, then you must show that the categories you deem so important are suitable to the discussion of truth wherever truth may exist. They can only be so if thinking beings exist essentially, and not merely *per accidens*, in social groups. You must show that for you too it takes two minds to make one, that the man without a fellow is not merely a possible imbecile but an impossible square-circle.

It is only on the assumption that the instrumentalist means to accept this challenge that I can suppose the problem of the man without a fellow to have more than a passing interest for him. But for the absolutist who makes the challenge, the lonely being of my imagining can not but be vital, has been vital throughout the history of absolutism, and should be more than ever vital to the absolutist of our day. For in spite of Mr. Dewey's claim upon the gratitude of posterity for the service rendered by instrumentalism in calling attention to the "social constitution of personal, even of private experience," I cannot think that posterity, supposing it to be duly grateful for the idea itself, will find much to choose between instrumentalist and absolutist in the matter of calling attention to the idea. Indeed, when I said that the image of the man without a fellow must be as critical for other philosophies as for my own, it was rather the absolutist than the instrumentalist I had in mind; for not only is it the central thesis of absolutism that the finite mind cannot exist save in fellowship with God, but it is to historic absolutism that we owe the first *Deduktion* of the dependence of finite mind on finite mind. And the absolutist of our day is no whit behind his forerunners in calling attention to the social reference of the most impersonal as well as of the most personal and private of our experiences,—for Professor Royce, nature itself is a social concept; nature is that in the description of which many men agree, in the moulding of which to their harmoniously different purposes many men coöperate.

So it has seemed to me that Mr. Dewey's claims for the service rendered by instrumentalism in "calling attention to" a doctrine that was old before we were young were *tant soit peu* exaggerated. The school that invented the theory has not abandoned it, has not spared emphasis in continuing to call attention to it, has outdone all others in the bold clearness with which it has set forth its meaning.

And yet this last statement of mine is perhaps in its turn an exaggeration. If there can be no doubt as to what a Fichte means to prove in the opening of his "Rechtslehre," there are whole chapters of Hegel's "Phaenomenologie" that leave me uncertain as to what they are intended to establish, and I am quite prepared to be told that my understanding of Mr. Royce's doctrine is a complete misunderstanding. When Mr. Royce speaks of nature as a "social concept" I have taken him to mean that a non-social being—a man without a fellow-man— would lack this concept; that a finite mind shut off from converse with other finite minds would be without any notion of a world in space and time, following mechanical laws and heaving with great rhythms. But such is the delicacy of the issue here involved that were Mr. Royce or another to tell me that he had no such meaning, but that his intention was merely to point out the extent to which we who are as a matter of fact social beings are influenced by that fact in our conception of all things —not merely in our ideas of property, credit, love, hate and such like mutalities, but in our notion of nature itself—if any one were to tell me this, I could not gainsay him with chapter and verse precluding such interpretation. I should be left trembling alone before the image of the man without a fellow, abandoned to the laying of my own ghost in my own way since for me alone is the portent.

But for me portent there would seem to be and the ghost must be faced if it can't be laid. In a number of papers addressed to this association in previous years, I have found myself maintaining a thesis that may best be defined in terms of what it denies. And what it denies is the spirit of Augustin's saying—"*Noli foras ire*—Go not out into the world; but return into thyself, for there in the inner man dwells truth." From this monkish sentence I have turned because I could find no way of getting at the truth about myself—even my innermost self—save by going abroad for it and receiving it as often as not at the hands of my fellows. It takes, I find myself having written,— it takes all the science of all the world to tell whether I am really in love as I think I am, whether I am really in pain as I take myself to be, whether I really see the color red as I sincerely assert that I do. No one familiar with the history of modern philosophy will find anything new or revolutionary in such utterances, though their import be to deny even to an idea any immediacy of meaning that is more than a relative immediacy, any truth that can be established without appeal to another. Such denial is sympathetic with the development of many modern idealisms and it antagonizes only such philosophies as starting with immediate data of consciousness—sensation or feeling—attempt to construct a world, a society of fellow-men, it may be a deity out of this data. What it accords with most intimately is that experience of life which one may have for the trouble of living. Is it a sound disjunction, that one who proclaims his love is either really a lover or really a liar? Is it true that laments are either final evidence of grief or proof of insincerity? Is the master of an art a convicted hypocrite when it is discovered that art for art's sake is not so surely the motive of his conduct but that, free to exercise his mastery to his heart's content, he does so in infinite discontent until recognition come his way? Is he not rather in his deepest heart uncertain of the truth about himself, of the reality of his mastery, until it is recognized, acknowledged, confirmed to him by another? In short, is there not that in the very meaning of truth which makes every truth depend upon an appeal to another?

And if this necessity of appeal is evident when the truth to be established by it concerns the most intimate and personal of private experiences, is it not all the more evident when there is question of the truth of ideas respecting nature? Whatever else we may think of those hard facts and inexorable laws which make up our image of a physical world, we always contemplate ourselves returning from the empirical study of them with our hands more firmly tied. But who or what is it that ties our hands? Part, at any rate, of the answer is to be read in that recurrent phrase of scientific literature: "So-and-so reports that he has obtained such-and-such results, but his observations remain unconfirmed by other experimenters." Experience so reported leaves our hands as uncomfortably free as before and we look to other observers to tighten our bonds for us.

It will readily be understood that this manner of reflection would leave me in closest sympathy with such utterances whether of instrumentalist or of absolutist as point out the dependence of an idea upon the appeal that it makes to another, and it was natural that I should have turned to these philosophers with my anxious question, But what if there be no other? What truth can there be for a man without a fellow-man to whom to appeal? Is it indeed true that my brother is so completely my keeper that without him I must dwindle and vanish? Their ways of answering these questions I must have imperfectly understood, for I find myself still addressing the same question to myself with what result the remainder of this paper shall set forth.

The situation from which we depart is in the nature of an antinomy. On the one hand we admit that a mind, to exist, must appeal to another; on the other we are not prepared to maintain that the conditions which bring into being such minds as we know, conditions of inheritance, education, intercommunication, are the only ones that could produce a mechanism reacting purposefully to the world about it. A first step toward the solution of this antinomy is clearly enough indicated, for if in order that we may attribute an idea to a finite being we must see to it that he is provided with another to whom to appeal, and if at the same time we place him in a situation that furnishes no Peter to his Paul, then we must regard this finite self as capable of being *its own other*.

I know that those who recognize in such a formula one of those amusing Hegelisms from the odd compulsion of which they have long since, praise God, emancipated themselves, will have nothing more to do with a "self that is its own other." But out of this situation I may be permitted to derive some amusement in my turn, for each of these emancipated ones is by way of congratulating himself on having become other than he was, without having ceased to be himself. And the truth of one's idea about Hegel will serve as well as any other example of truth to illustrate my meaning when I say that the finding of truth is indeed an appeal, an intercommunication between points of view; but every man, however complete his social isolation, is himself a society of points of view. If indeed he live with other men, their point of view respecting any truth, even one touching most intimately himself, his own emotions, his own mastery, may be worth as much as his own; but if he live by himself, his own other points of view may be depended on to try out his present opinion—we say that he may *change his mind*. The first condition of there being a mind is simply a situation in which there is room enough for a change of mind; instead of Fichte's formula, No man without a fellow, I should conclude, No mind without a change of mind.

I am not sure whether the instrumentalist would accept this interpretation of his category of "social reference"; but it is certain the absolutist would not be done with me if I were to let matters drop here. He would lose no time in pointing out that our troubles were not over, but only fairly begun. "If," he would say, "truth involves an appeal from one point of view to another, which point of view holds the truth and how are we to know it? An appeal to truth is something more than a polite conversation between different view-points content to remain in such agreement or disagreement as their intercourse reveals." He would ask this question knowing full well that my answer must be, No point of view holds the truth, nor does any finite group of actually expressed opinions give us a way of calculating the truth. And to come at once to the point to which the absolutist would have me come, I may as well admit that the series of points of view to which we must appeal for the truth of the most private of our meanings is essentially infinite. "Then," the absolutist would argue, "some of these points of view, and of course an infinity of them, must be merely possible points of view?" The confession that such is my understanding of the case would probably end his interest in the matter, for absolutism might well enough be defined as the philosophy that flees from an infinite series to take refuge in an infinite mind. But from this very definition it follows that it is not from the infinite the absolutist flees; he would distinguish between infinities and would represent himself as delivered from the bad infinite by an acknowledging of the good. Now the bad infinite is one that endlessly loses itself in bare possibilities —in bare possibilities that are for him impossible. He flees from infinite to infinite indeed, but from the possible infinite in which meaning is lost to the actual infinite in which meaning is realized.

With all the absolutist's criticism of the category of possibility I find myself in close accord. If I judge a proposition to be possibly true, it is because its contradictory does not follow from certain premises presupposed. Often enough these premises are tacitly presupposed, and then we have the illusion that we are dealing with pure possibilities; but this is only illusion, the premises are there or the possibility is not there—take these actualities away and the posibility left on our hands is indeed too bare for presentation. Against the danger of falling into a way of thinking in terms of bare possibilities, I would be as anxious as the absolutist to protect myself, and if I have escaped from an antinomy to fall into the pit of "permanent possibilities" I ask no one to join me there—the place is uncomfortably full and full of discomfort.

But while the absolutist's caution against bare possibilities is wise and admirable, his precaution against them is exaggerated. It is not enough for him to be assured that there is a core of actuality to an infinite series, he must be assured that it is actual in all its endlessness. Most of us, however, find no difficulty in handling an infinite whose law is given in a finite number of terms—and not merely *some* finite number, but a perfectly definite finite number. Such a series is that of the integral numbers, whose law is given as soon as the phrase "and so on," with which any such law must end, is meaningful and unambiguous. But this phrase does become meaningful and unambiguous after the two equations, $1+1=2$, $2+1=3$ are written down; then and not till then is the third equation defined to be $3+1=4$. Since the series in infinite, no one can construct all of its terms without accomplishing a contradiction; but the terms that remain at any given time unconstructed are no bare possibilities; their possibility is a logical consequence of actually given premises, finite and definite in number.

The bearing of these reflections upon the nature of that infinite series of points of view to which an idea must appeal for its truth and meaning is obvious enough. I have said that there could be no mind without a change of mind; let me put the result in another and more definite form: It takes two points of view to make one, and both of these points of view must be guaranteed as actual before that infinite series can be constructed, without an appeal to which no truth can be defined, no idea can have meaning.

Of the minimal situation which permits of ascribing an idea to any perceiver we may now draw a preliminary picture. This attribution is made by an onlooker A whose world contains a perceiver B, and the object C of B's perception. It is essential to this situation that the perceiver B should himself be perceived; for "it takes two points of view to make one." As for the object C of this perception, it is doubtless inaccurate to speak of it as though it existed ready-made in A's world; my meaning is that this world contains the actual material out of which the notion of an object may be constructed. Suppose B to be observed in the act of measuring the length of a rod. A, the onlooker, calls this measurement "B's idea" of the length of the rod. In doing so he contrasts this single measurement with a series whose average, as the series progresses, is subject to a decreasing probable error and freed from one source after another of constant error. Without the data and the method for constructing this series, object and idea lose their meaning together. The onlooker A sees clearly that the series is infinite, but there is enough that is actual to define this infinite and to keep its unrealized terms from becoming bare possibilities.

Nor is this infinite reference of the idea to other points of view the only series that develops from our minimal situation. The onlooker A takes to heart the lesson he has learned from watching, commenting on, and defining B's idea and its object. From a new point of view he applies the result to the former situation. His world with B in it, a highway of truth stretching out before him, becomes itself the idea of a world. The philosopher sees his old self part of a new world, and in this world his old self stands in its turn facing an infinite highway at the end of which lies the truth about B's idea and the object of B's idea. A second infinite series is defined, but like the first it grows out of hard actualities and its possibilities are not bare.

In this analysis the *otherness* of the standpoints that I have called A's and B's, the onlooker's and the perceiver's, is a matter of definition; the *otherness* of the men who occupy these standpoints is an historical accident. My man without a fellow might occupy both, for such is the nature of the self that it can well enough be its own other. Nor do I see that a mind so isolated need be limited in its possibilities. True, a hundred men can build a house more quickly than one, but if that one happen to be a genius he might—give him time—build a finer house. Just so our dependence upon neighbors for the acquisition of knowledge is a question of speed; give him time and it all depends upon the manner of man he is whether our man without a fellow turn out imbecile or creator.

In view of these reflections, is the importance attached by the instrumentalist to his social categories altogether justified? I do not say that they are less significant than the categories exploited by absolutists; for if I have gone so far as to maintain that the man without a fellow will not be lost for lack of a brother-hand to guide him, I must go to the extent of denying that he will need the everlasting arms to uphold him. In which conclusion I find a certain interest, for I have suspected at times that our lonely figure was less a homeless ghost than the silent-working being who dwells deep down under the familiar, convivial, social surface of each one of us.

PART TWO

EMPIRICAL IDEALISM

SENSATION AND THE DATUM OF
SCIENCE

IX.

SENSATION AND THE DATUM OF SCIENCE

Die einfache Unmittelbarkeit ist selbst ein Reflexionsausdruck, und bezieht sich auf den Unterschied von dem Vermittelten.—Hegel.

THE aspect of scientific thought most generally insisted upon emphasizes what might be called its constructive function. I say constructive, for when on the basis of certain "given" experiences science erects a law that is to be exemplified in all possible experiences, it may, I think, appropriately be said to construct a world out of certain data. It is, for example, on this constructive aspect of our thought we are accustomed to lay stress, whenever we wax enthusiastic over the spectacle of scientific progress. To have inferred from our experiences on this little globe the structure of distant stars, to have divined from the behavior of our gross surroundings the dance of molecules and the play of atoms, to have forced mute rocks and earth-strata to tell the history of a geological past, to have derived from the phenomenon of wasted heat some notion of a solar system's destiny,—these are some of the achievements rightly or wrongly attributed to science in any popular account of its progress. It is the contrast between the meagerness of the facts and the vastness of the structure built upon them, the remoteness of its boundaries, that takes hold on the general imagination. Nor wrongly, for science has accomplished, if not perhaps just these, yet equally difficult feats presenting a similar constructive aspect.

Natural, however, and justifiable as such a view of the function of science may seem to be, one of the terms in which it is expressed has long been felt to conceal a certain difficulty. I do not now refer to the skeptical doubts that have existed from the earliest time respecting the justification of inference. It is unnecessary to consider them here; partly because, granting the logical consistency of a position that would deprive our thinking of all certainty, yet science would receive little hurt from the recognition of the risk it ran with every step of its progress; but more because the difficulty to which I refer lies deeper than all that skepticism points out. For while the latter may doubt our ability to pass from what is given to what is not given, yet it universally accords a meaning to, and very generally invests its little residue of confidence in, the immediately present experience. The query with which we are here concerned, however, does not rest with that. It challenges, not the truth only, but the very meaning of thought by asking: What, pray, *is* "given" in experience? What is the datum of science? Taken in connection with the commonsense view of the constructive function of science here presented, it would seem to have a meaning to ask: What is the starting point of our thought? Nay, it would seem to be absolutely necessary that we should be able to answer such a question, and that one could not escape paradox were one to doubt whether such a "given" element of experience could be found. Yet one who experiences difficulty in finding it is in the best of company, and one who puts it beyond finding is not alone.

However natural it may seem to suppose that one can at once point to the facts with which one's thinking starts, yet, historically, most attempts to do so have proved abortive. That "mere fact" presented, has been shown to include some element of the constructive or inferential, to be not really "given," but rather "taken." And so the method of search for the given element of experience has resolved itself into progressive attempts to abstract from certain definable products of our thought, the constructive elements they have been found to con-

SENSATION AND THE DATUM OF SCIENCE

tain. Our first effort must be to follow this empirical method to its logical conclusion.

A single illustration will stand for all first steps in such a search; the reasoning is perfectly familiar. The physicist, for example, quite generally represents himself as starting with matter and force, or with matter and energy. "Matter," says Thomson and Tait, "is that which can be perceived by the senses, or is that which can be acted upon by, or can exert force. . . . Force is a direct object of sense, probably of all our senses, and certainly of the 'muscular sense.'"[1] Yet a very little reflection will convince one that neither matter nor force is immediately given in experience. For "matter," characterized by mass, "force," by accelerated motion, are terms which have a meaning only when used to describe a *universal* way of behaving on the part of bodies placed in relation to each other. No isolated instance of bodies in motion would give rise to the concept of mass and force. It must be a *law* which they express; it *is* a law which physicists use them to express. And with its necessary universality, a law is not an immediate datum.[2]

[1] *Treatise on Natural Philosophy*, § 297.

[2] I offer this illustration for what it is worth, and if any one claim that matter and force are not the physicist's starting point, but rather his ending point, I should be willing to admit that they were as often the latter as the former. Indeed, one of the authors (Tait) above quoted as pointing out the immediacy of

Taking another step, one might be tempted to say that if bodies in motion were not in their immediacy expressive of mass and force, yet merely as bodies occupying different places at different times, they might be observed as so many facts.

Not so, however, for the space and time factors involved are not in any sense immediately given, and at least they cannot stand for the merely present experience. Leaving out the motion, there remains then the body; that at least we can at any moment observe? But again, it does not require the keenness of a Hume to see that a body cannot all be presented at once, but that out of what is presented the concept of the body arises from inferences based on past experience. On past experiences of what? And here we come to what is usually regarded as the final stage of our journey. That which is, at each moment, merely given; that out of which, as moment is added to moment, the concept of the body, of its motion, of the whole

our knowledge of matter and force, does not hesitate to say: "We do not know, and probably are incapable of discovering what matter is." But although it is hard to see how both notions of matter can live peaceably together in the same mind, yet every student of philosophy is familiar with the spectacle of fire and water abiding on brotherly terms, if only there be a little insulating space between them. And so I can readily admit that physicists hold a view of matter and force quite contradictory to that which I have ascribed to them. It is not less true that they hold this view also.

complex universe of matter and force is constructed, —that datum for which we seek, can be nothing other than the immediately given sense-impression. From Hume, who would have all the world of our beliefs to be founded on the vivid impression of sense,[1] to Ernst Mach, who proclaims the world to be made up of sensations,[2] the regressive search for what is merely given in experience has with remarkable unanimity on the part of the seekers stopped at sense-impressions.

From such illustrations as the foregoing, it would seem that science, beside the constructive function first pointed out, is presented with quite as real a problem of a destructive kind, and that its advance is to be measured quite as much by its regress in the latter direction as by its progress in the former. So far from the given element of experience being that about which science need ask no questions, so far from it being that which, in answer to an ill-considered question, may be simply pointed at, it seems to be that respecting which we could put the problem of science in an exactly inverted form: Not here is it required of science out of the "given" to construct a "world," but rather, out of the "world" to construct a "given." When one has wondered enough at the growing remoteness of

[1] *Treatise*, Bk. I, p. 3, Sec. 6, 7.
[2] *Analysis of Sensation*, Introduction, Sec. 5.

scientific "constructs," one may turn to admire the progressive intimacy of scientific "destructs," if I may coin the term.

In the face of this historic paradox I propose quite baldly the following theses, as anticipating the outcome of our study: (1) that sensation does not and cannot stand for an immediate datum of experience; (2) that no other term will stand for it; (3) that the method generally followed never will allow us to attach a meaning to the "given" factor of experience. If these be made to appear, it will be time to re-examine our statement of the problem, for in that must lie the cause of our embarrassment.

"Sensation" Not Immediate

In support of the first point, it might be sufficient to show that, in general, we neither define nor use "sensation" in a way consistent with the ideal of immediacy. Or if, perchance, one do so define it, one still will not use it so.

For example, from the days of Hobbes—not to go further back—to those of the most recent writers on the subject (*e. g.*, Meinong), sensation is constantly defined as a mental state dependent upon a physical stimulus and a physiological structure. In addition, the so-called properties of sensation (quality, intensity, and local sign) are named, defined, and used in a way implying certain relations to the physical world and to the physiological organism. Of course, if these psycho-physical and psycho-physiological relationships form part of the *meaning* of sensation (and if they do not, why should they appear in the definition?), it is quite impossible to know a sensation without possessing and using all the complex concepts implied in the recognition of these relationships. To possess and to know a sensation is, then, far from possessing and knowing a simple and immediate datum.

To be sure, the remark any one defending the immediacy of sensation would here be tempted to make is this: That to possess a sensation and to know a sensation; to have an experience that *is* a sensation and to recognize an experience one has to be a sensation, are quite different matters. The sensation itself may be simple and immediate, one's knowledge of it may be complex and inferential.

I cannot here display at length the fallacy I believe to underlie the use to which the distinction between what a thing is, and what it is taken to be, is ordinarily put. Scarcely a product of philosophic thought, from the most transcendent *ens rationis* to the most intimate immediate, but illustrates an abuse of the principle. Suffice it to say, many have pointed out that we cannot thus separate the existence of a thing (even though that thing be a mental state or "idea"), from the recognition of it. It will not do at one time to cry with a loud voice, "the *esse* of things is *percipi*," and at another to proclaim that a sensation may *be* without *being known*, or may be known without being recognized as a sensation. To use Shadworth Hodgson's pithy inelegance, "a thing *is* what it *is known as*," and certainly the converse is equally true, "a thing *isn't* what it *is not known as*."

There is, of course, a meaning in the distinction between knowing a thing and knowing about a thing. Every day we use phrases implying such a distinction. The fact was thus and so, we say, but was not known to be so. Meaning such a distinction certainly has; but for whom? Evidently, only for one who has the broader knowledge, the recognition, in question. Only for such a standpoint *did* a state of affairs exist without being recognized. But also, from this standpoint, the recognition is not merely possible, but is actual. The *esse* which was not to be *percipi*, turns out to be one kind of *percipi* as distinguished from another. Any attempt to escape from the actual recognition upon which the meaning of a thing rests, in favor of existence as standing for the mere possibility of recognition, will lead us to absurdities of which the "thing-in-itself" is the standard example. To call the "thing" in question an "idea" does not alter the case. It is not the "thing," but the "in-itself" that is the source of danger in the phrase. As Bradley has put it: "Mere possibility is impossible."

In the case in point then, the sensation must be all that constructive product which its definition implies. The attempt to regard it as immediate, in the face of its ordinary definition, must fail. But I say, further, that if we give up the ordinary meaning of sensation, and define the term solely by the condition that it shall stand for the simple and immediate datum of experience, we cannot long use it consistently with our definition. For if it is to remain a term in any vocabulary, it must be a term of social intercourse, by the use of which one may convey to another the meaning one intends. I need not point out that in all our scientific investigations we asume sensations to be communicable, and those of different individuals to be comparable. We mean something, for example, when we say that certain sensations of the color-blind are different from those of the normal subject. In order that we may mean something by such a statement, it is necessary that our view of sensation do not rob it of its describable and expressible nature. When, however, we define sensation as the immediate datum of experience, we must deny it to be one of those products of social experience the description of which is verifiable by all; different descriptions of which are comparable by all. We make sensation the peculiar and incommunicable possession of each individual consciousness.

From the time of Gorgias to the present day, the question has been constantly cropping up to our discomfort: What reason can we have for supposing the sensations of others to be like (or, in certain cases, to be different from) our own? Evidently by our descriptive expressions we do not really convey to each other our immediate consciousness on the subject. It requires more daring than most of us possess, to follow to its logical end Max Muller's identification of thought and language. As a makeshift we fall back on that flimsy "analogy hypothesis." We treat sensations in other minds as ejects, and frankly admit the assumption of relations of likeness and difference existing between the sensations of others and our own sensations to be quite beyond verification. I would that I had space to raise the question as to whether it has any meaning to make such an assumption. Certainly I should begin by asking whether likeness and difference could subsist between immediates, and particularly between immediates belonging to worlds expressly supposed never to be the common property of a single point of view. And if our question were answered in the negative, we should be led to relegate the concept of "ejects" to the limbo of "rejects." Meanwhile, I may perhaps have said enough to indicate the way in which, if we define sensation as an immediate datum, we must proceed to violate our definition so soon as we regard sensations as communicable, as products of a social experience. If, on the other hand, we cling to such a definition, and give up our demand for articulateness, then, like Cratylus, we can merely wag the finger and hold our peace.

"Quality" Not Immediate

But this remark belongs rather to the discussion of our second thesis. For we have suggested that not only is the experience we ordinarily call "a sensation" no merely immediate datum, but that we cannot attach to the term any more recondite meaning apt to satisfy our demand for an immediate.

Modern psychologists generally have not failed to see that a difficulty is contained in any view of sensation which regards it as an immediate datum. They are, for the most part, agreed that sensation so viewed could no longer mean a sound, or a color, or anything else it has meant or may now mean in the language of common-sense. A certain compromise is frequently attempted, which consists in stripping sensation of its so-called properties, thus forcing it to stand for "mere quality." Helmholtz, for instance, proposes, in the cause of immediacy, the following criterion of sensation: "No sensation indubitably present could be set aside and destroyed by an act of the understanding; hence, nothing in our sense perceptions is to be recognized as a sensation which, by momenta evidently derived from past experience, can be corrected in perception and changed into its opposite."[1] In other words, a sensation pure and simple must involve no judgment based on past experience and liable to error, but must be immediately known and recognized. One is not surprised when one finds the application of this criterion driving Helmholtz to the conclusion that "only the qualities of sensation are to be regarded as really pure sensation."

This step taken by Helmholtz marks an inevitable stage in the progress toward a mere datum. It illustrates the method whose historical applications we have been tracing. As soon, that is, as a certain term has been found to include judgment or construction, its immediacy vanishes. Rejecting the constructive elements, the portion remaining on our hands then serves as the immediate datum—it alone is the *unzweifelhaft-gegenwärtige Empfindung*. It illustrates, too, the continual failure of attempts to compromise between the demand for immediacy and the demand for describability. From the "last seeming" of Protagoras to the "sense-im-

[1] *Physiologische Optik*, 2 A. p. 610f.

pression" of Hume, the history of philosophic reflection presents one series of attempts to chase the starting point of thought inward, and yet to retain an ability to tell what that starting point is. The "mere quality" of Helmholtz may, perhaps, stand for the last term of such a series; but it must fail, like its predecessors, to meet both demands.

For criticism must take the same form in treating of quality, as it did in dealing with the supposedly richer term, sensation. Quality, too, if it is to stand for a mere datum, loses first its ordinary meaning, then all possible meaning; whereas if it is to retain meaning, it fails to fulfil the conditions of a merely present experience. For, like the more complex term sensation, the term quality of sensation stands in ordinary use for a psycho-physical and psycho-physiological conception. Our obvious motive for calling certain differences of sensation "qualitative," is to distinguish them from local and intensive differences. So that, ordinarily at least, quality is not a genus of which intensity and local sign are species, but all three are rather coördinate species. As such, their differentiæ are usually stated in psycho-physical terms; but even where this is not so, they must be mutually dependent for their meaning.

Still, I confess, it is not uncommon to make quality a more generic term than the others mentioned. Thus it is frequently claimed that all memtal differences are qualitative, all physical differences quantitative. I do not know what truth there may be in this proposition, regarded as a statement of fact, after one has defined qualitative and quantitative differences. As it stands, it has the air of offering itself as a definition of these terms. If so, it is evident that one could not hope to distinguish between mental and physical differences until one was able to attach meaning to the physical and mental worlds, a meaning which, I fancy, can lay little claim to immediacy. A definition of qualitative difference in these terms would make quality a highly reflective product, not at all an immediate datum.

If, as a last alternative, one drop the adjective "mental," and define qualitative difference as mere difference; even then it is the experience of *differents* which gives rise to the concept of quality. *A quality* could not then be immediate, and if one should claim that *qualities,* including all their differences, might be so, it is difficult to see how the manifoldness of such an experience could be realized without comparison with other experiences which it in part resembled and from which it in part differed. To say, as Bradley does, that qualities and relations can, under proper conditions, be present, but not recognized, is in violation of his

SENSATION AND THE DATUM OF SCIENCE

own most cherished principles.[1] It is exactly that divorcement of existence and recognition, an elevation of "mere possibility" into a place of dignity among meaningful concepts, which he generally condemns with such force and skill in the theories of others.

But further dwelling on this point would not be helpful. Suffice it to say that in proportion as one abstracts from judgments and inferences referring to experiences, possible, but not actual, one abstracts from meaning. So that if one has carried the method far enough to retain nothing that is not immediately given, one must have succeeded in getting rid of all meaning—which, of course, is not the conclusion we wished for. The method must in the end make the immediate quite inarticulate—hence the introductory allusion to Cratylus.

Nothing of what has thus far been said in support of the thesis that sensation could not stand for an immediate, however its meaning be modified, is new. It is even urged with the greatest clearness by those who still insist upon regarding sensation as the given fact of consciousness upon which all constructive thought must be based. It merely serves, however, to suggest to such a new subtlety in their attitude toward sensation. For, having rec-

[1] *Appearance and Reality*, pp. 105, 159, 225, 459.

ognized that the very nature of our demand for the immediately given must contradict that of our demand for something stateable and describable, the next step is to make the immediate a mere ideal, a limit to the process of abstraction from inference. And this goal, unattainable though it is, they cannot forego calling *a sensation!*

Such a position is the final attainment of modern subtlety. The somewhat intangible nature of the conclusion permits it to escape the criticisms to which franker, if also grosser, statements would fall victims. This vagueness would militate against the standpoint, were it not that our ordinary attitude toward constructive thought seemed absolutely to demand some conclusion respecting the problem of the datum of experience, while criticism had claimed simpler attempts as its prey. From these motives, perhaps, not a few of our modern psychologists stand on this ground. For example, Wundt, after having defined sensation as a simple mental element, goes on to say: "The concept of sensation, so defined, proceeds merely from the needs of our psychological analysis. The simple sensation is never given alone, but is the result of an abstraction."[1]

[1] *Grungzüge*, 3A, I, p. 289. In this, and in the following illustration, it might be claimed that the search for a simple element of consciousness, and that for an immediate datum of thought, were not identical. The former object of search might

SENSATION AND THE DATUM OF SCIENCE

More explicitly still, James pictures the outcome of mental analysis as an endless process of abstraction. It is, he says, "never complete, the analysis of a compound never perfect, because we can never approach a compound with the image in our mind of any one of its components in a perfectly pure form. Colors, sounds, smells, are just as much entangled with other matter as are more formal elements of experience, such as extension, intensity, effort, pleasure, difference, likeness, harmony, badness, strength, and even consciousness itself. All are embedded in one world. But by the fluctuations and permutations of which we have spoken, we come to form a pretty good notion of the *direction* in which each element differs from the rest, and so we frame the notion of it as a *terminus*, and continue to mean it as an individual thing. . . . At bottom the process is one of *conception*, and is everywhere, even in the sphere of simple sensible qualities, the same as that by which we are usually understood to attain to the notions of ab-

be an abstraction, while the latter could not be so without contradiction. But, although the form given to the problem may influence the associations connected with it (as when Wundt compares the psychologist's need of elements with the chemist's demand for atoms), yet in the end they both present the same characteristic attempt to eliminate construction. With both authors cited (as with Hume), sensation generally plays the rôle of an immediate datum, although here it seems the most remote abstraction.

stract goodness, perfect felicity, absolute power and the like: the direct perception of the difference between compounds, and the imaginary prolongation of the direction of the difference to an ideal terminus, the notion of which we fix and keep as one of our permanent subjects of discourse."[1]

I do not know of any other attempt to set forth the method by which we arrive at that most puzzling conception, "an element of consciousness," that so gets at the nerve of the problem as does this one. And yet it is a complete change of attitude, if we compare it with the statements of a Hobbes, Condillac, or Hume. The sense impression, so far from being our datum, has become an *ideal terminus* of abstraction. We should change our old formula to read, *nihil est in sensu quod non fuerit in intellectu.* The position that seemed most natural at first, seems most untenable in the end. And yet the immediacy of sensation is no chance guess. Every one must at one time or another have thought it unquestionable that the most intimate of all his possessions were his present sensations. Yes, Professor James himself, although he here seems to regard a complex and highly reflective world as the starting point of analysis, and therefore as the immediate datum, does not always hold this view. It is one of his most fundamental habits of thought

[1] *Psychology,* Vol. 1, p. 508 (Abridged).

to let the starting point of all mental construction be immediately given, perfectly simple. Thus we find him saying *"there is no manifold of coexisting ideas; the notion of such a thing is a chimera. Whatever things are thought in relation are thought from the outset in a unity, in a single pulse of subjectivity, a single psychosis, feeling or state of mind."*[1] These two attitudes may not be ultimately contradictory, but respecting the simple element of consciousness they assert exactly opposite things, and they present the task of reconciliation in no equivocal form.

"Immediate" Can Have No Name

Sensation, in the series of changes through which we have followed it in the course of our search for a datum, has at last come to stand for little more than the name of a problem. It no longer answers, but merely expresses, our demand for an immediate datum of experience. It gives, so to speak, the sanction of its name to a demand which it admits must remain eternally unsatisfied. Now it is perhaps a matter of taste whether we shall, with Wundt, rob the term sensation of its common and useful meaning, to impose upon it a function no term can perform with credit; that, namely, of standing for a mere abstraction. It is safe to say

[1] *Psychology*, Vol. I, p. 278.

SENSATION AND THE DATUM OF SCIENCE

that no one, least of all Wundt, long continues to use the term in this, to say the least, highly technical sense.

But it is no longer a matter of taste as to whether we ought to apply any name to, or retain any such concept as, a datum of constructive thought, which not only is not given, but can never be found after the most vigorous search. When we recognize sensation to be only one of many terms having stood for the immediate datum (among which are to be mentioned the sensible world of Plato, of Indian philosophy, and of mediæval asceticism; the human, the individual world, or the "last seeming" of Protagoras; the solipsistic world of Gorgias; the present happiness of the Cyrenaics; the *ego* of Descartes; the *Empfindung, Eindruck, Vortellung, Gegenstand* of Kant; the vivid sense-impressions of Hume; the colors, sounds, odors, etc., of Hobbes, Locke, and Condillac; the mere quality of Helmholtz)—when, I say, we recognize that *anything* may be taken as immediately given under the influence of a proper contrast (usually an historical accident), we begin to ask whether to a series of this kind there should or could be a limit—even an "ideal limit." We wonder whether the concept of the datum of science is not a purely relative one, arising from the contrast of the more constructive to the less constructive terms of our thought; whether the pure immediate is not a vain idol, erected to satisfy a demand that ought not to exist and failing of satisfaction *because* it ought not to exist: the demand, namely, for a starting point of all thought.

If we answer this question in the affirmative, we should, once for all, banish from our thought the concept of a mere datum; and, what is of practical interest to the psychologist, we should cease to prostitute our useful term "sensation" to the function of standing for an unattainable and, to all appearances, unnecessary abstraction. If not, we are faced with the paradox that the starting point of science, the "given" out of which it is to construct its world, the indubitably present as opposed to the inferred, that this starting point has become —what? An unattainable ideal! Surely no better illustration could be given of that spectacle of our thinking Hegel so quaintly calls *"die verkehrte Welt."*

We have now followed sensation through its various attempts to play the rôle of an immediate datum. Although sensation has perhaps been more seriously considered as a satisfactory solution of the problem than has any other term, yet, if we are right, it is more or less accidental as to which of the many terms having laid claim to immediacy one selects as one's point of attack. It must have become clear that the *a posteriori* method we have so far pursued could be turned with equal effect against any other proposed immediate datum.

And now, how can we be sure *a priori* that a mere datum can never be found? Evidently we can be so only in case the concept prove self-contradictory. And this seems, indeed, to be the case; for to find a thing is to describe it or define it; but an immediate is, by the very conditions it must fulfil to be such, indescribable and indefinable. This might be made to appear in many ways, but all of them would seem to depend upon one principle, namely: that description can be effected only by the use of universals; the thing described must be regarded as a type; but to be a type is to be one of an indefinite number of possible similar individuals forming a class; hence, to regard a thing as a type requires the possibility of passing in thought beyond what is given; and this is inconsistent with immediacy. Implied in this relation of likeness which is essential to description, is also the relation of difference. In the old Aristotelian phrase, the differentia is just as important to description as is the proximate genus. From this point of view also, relationship to what is not given is essential to the description of any "given thing. Hence, so long as we regard that thing as describable, it is not "merely" given.

All this is so evident, it might well appear surprising that anyone should attempt to advance any definable term as standing for the immediate datum of thought. And, inevitably, one who does so is driven through various stages of changing the meaning of such a term, until it sinks into mere inanity. It is just this that drives one to the position of regarding the datum as a mere ideal. But, if the datum is a mere ideal, what is the superstructure raised upon it? It is this question that drives one back again to seek for a starting point at once solid and stateable. Apparently one is in the position of saying that we cannot start until we have already proceeded, we cannot proceed until we have started.

Restatement

I accompanied the statement of the theses foredooming all search for an immediately given element of experience, with the remark that if we failed to find the starting point our ordinary view of the nature of thought seemed to demand, we must proceed to a new statement of our problem; *i. e.*, attain to a new view of the function of that body of observation and reflection which, in its systematized form, we call science. Let us attempt this:

We started out with the view that the function of science was constructive. In order that such construction might proceed, it seemed necessary for it to secure some absolute starting point, a mere datum, or mere data. When, however, we took any chance product of this constructive process, and by getting rid of all factors depending on inference or judgment, tried to find that from which it could have started, it seemed to be clear, not only that actually we could find no beginning, but that theoretically we ought to expect to find none.

Now the thought naturally presents itself that our trouble lies in a failure to state the problem of science in terms experienced enough to distinguish between the kind of starting point our reflection must have, and the ultimate data for construction to which we neither must nor can attain. And I do not know but what the difficulty is removed beyond troubling, if we hold that the function of science is neither constructive, as we first thought it to be, nor destructive, as the attempt fully to express this constructive aspect forced us to be, but rather reconstructive. Only as such must it have an absolute starting point, and that starting point is the one which the history of thought indicates to us: the whole common-sense world in which we find ourselves when we begin to "reflect." When we become scientific, our problem is to reconstruct such a world, a process involving both analysis and synthesis. With respect to any given stage of the process of reconstruction, the basis, a group of facts, is indeed said to be "given"; but is given for the construction in question, and by the point of view from which the reconstruction is attempted. As elsewhere stated, they are "taken" as a starting point, and are just as essentially a *result* of analysis as they are the *assumptions* of synthesis.

From the standpoint here occupied, it is no longer surprising that history should present us with so varied a list of proposed "immediates." Each was generated under the influence of an attempt to construct something out of it. The "world of sense" was simply "the world" of common-sense, until Plato tried to construct out of it his world of Ideas. And that he should have attempted such a construction, was simply an effort to reconstruct the world of common-sense so that it should be intelligible and devoid of the contradictions his reflection discovered in it. So in Kant, the *Anschauung*, the *Gegenstand*, the *Empfindung*, in turn play the part of *das Gegebene*, according to the aspect of *Erfahrung* that he is trying to reconstruct. Again, it is owing to a failure to recognize the essentially double nature of reconstructive thought that we all of us, like James, now emphasize the simplicity of immediate experience and the complexity which reflection develops in it (or out of it), while anon we insist upon the complexity of

SENSATION AND THE DATUM OF SCIENCE

the world with which we start and the highly reflective or constructive nature of what simple elements of that world as we would struggle to win. Finally, I am reminded of the striking passage with which Hegel introduces the *Lehre vom Seyn:* "Only in modern times has it been recognized that there is a certain difficulty in finding a starting point in philosophy, and the reason for this difficulty, together with the possibility or removing it, has been variously set forth. The starting point of philosophy must be either mediate or immediate, and it is easy to show that it can be neither the one nor the other: and so the one and the other way of beginning find their refutation."[1] The reader may judge how far the present analysis expresses and removes this difficulty.

Our positive conclusion then is this: That we should find it necessary to institute a search for that which is given to start with, is a stateable condition of affairs only in case we can distinguish between the sense in which our search must start, and that in which *a* starting point is its goal. And this possibility seems to be realized by considering the function of science to be reconstructive. The starting point for reconstruction we must indeed have; but it is no simple datum for construction. A comparatively simple datum for construc-

[1] *Logik*, p. 55.

tion we must indeed take; but it is not the starting point, it is rather one assumed ending point of our scientific labor. An absolutely simple and ultimate datum we neither must nor can have. Our search for it is a search for what, if found, would put an end to our scientific progress in the direction of further reconstruction.

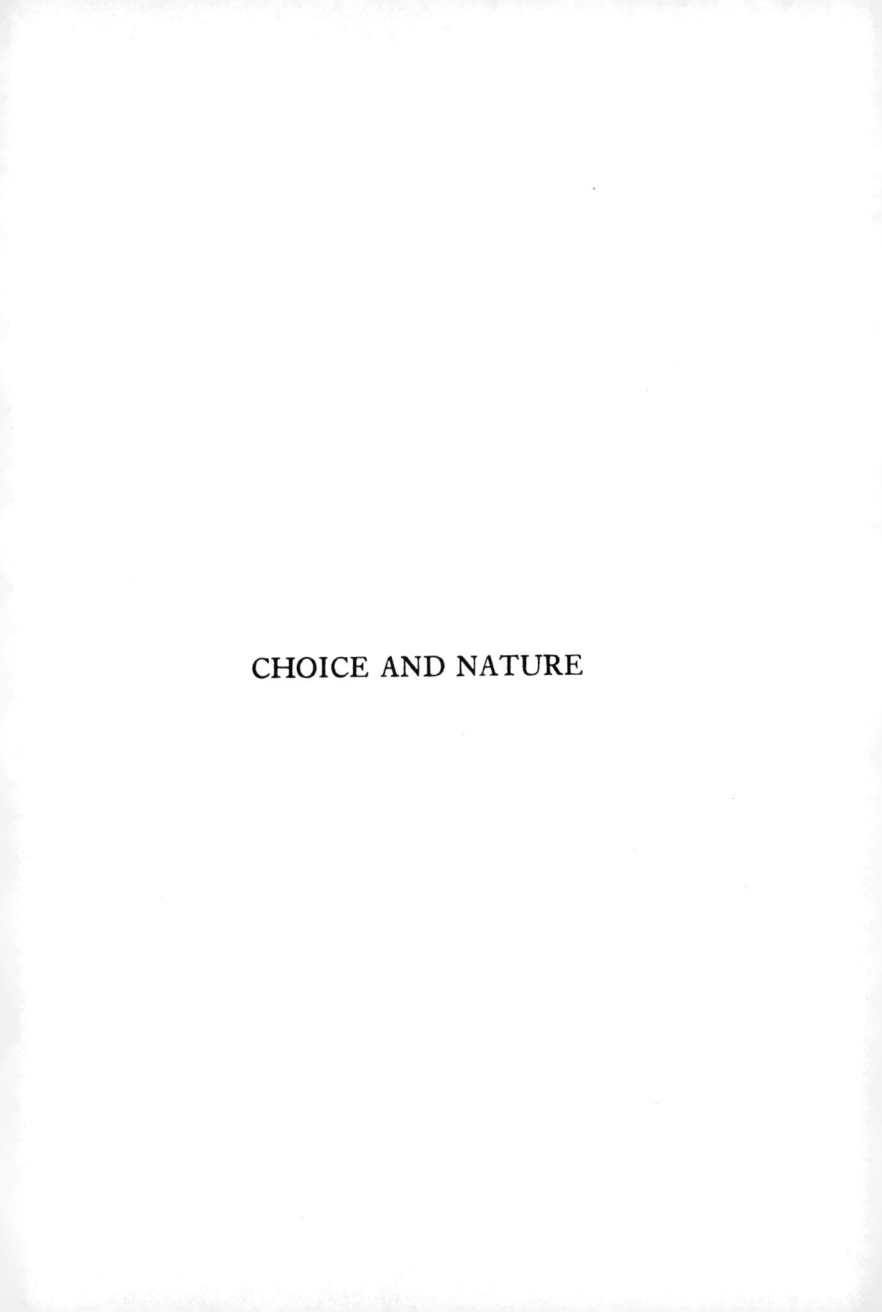

CHOICE AND NATURE

X.

CHOICE AND NATURE

1. *Method.*—In so experienced an age one can hardly beguile oneself into a sense of the newness of one's reflections. It is with something of regret for a bygone freshness that Lucretius's eager lines come back to us:—

> *"iuvat integros accedere fontis*
> *atque haurire, iuvatque novos decerpere flores."*

Nor has the pleasant weariness of completed labors taken the place of the beginner's zest. We can count scarce one question settled, one finished task: our philosophic inheritance is a tangle of opinion, to unravel which is a labor greater than all the rest. Yet if the past is to repay in enlightenment what it has cost in disillusionment we must *make* it teach us. This is our modern problem, and the nature of the task has, to some extent, dictated the method of its accomplishment.

The history of philosophy is in itself a philosophy, and to develop its method has been the first interest of our century. Finding conflicting opinion, this philosophy has sought underlying motives, and giving play to motives, it has enticed conflict into contrast. Dwelling on antitheses, it has forced history to take on a dialectic form, and in expressing the truth grasped, has pointed neither to extremes of doctrine nor to "happy means," but to the continuous unfolding of the story. Thus it has made use of the very discord of opinion to teach the lesson of experience, and as part of the lesson learned has ceased to be anxious for the fate of its "last word." It is in the spirit of such a method that I would approach the old problem of the relation of Choice to Nature: it is because the problem is so old that I venture to attack it.

2. *Progress, Determinism and Tolerance.*—To begin as far back as we may: the more primitive the intelligence we examine, the more we find it impressed with the caprice of detail in Nature, and the more ready does it show itself to see in this lawlessness the play of imagined choices. To the savage,—yes, to the cultivated Greek (and perhaps to the larger portion of the civilized world today) —it is not only fellow-man and fellow-animal that behaves in an unpredictable way, but the tossed divining stick, the trickling blood of the sacrifice, the tea-leaf floating in the cup. These seeming chances are interpreted as choices: they are given an oracular meaning, and are not one with that routine in which the stone always falls to the ground, the arrow always flies toward the mark. On the other

hand, the farther back we go in civilization, the less room do we find set apart for the play of opinion. A statement is either true or false, an action good or bad; there is a vanishingly small region within which different interpretations of the same facts are allowed to abide together in peace. In a word, primitive thought is at once fanciful and intolerant.

Progress is understood gradually to invert this state of affairs. With expanding science the region of indeterminateness shrinks, with growing experience reflection is forced to admit many interpretations of the same range of phenomena; choice vanishes from the midst of Nature described and reappears in the function of description. Science and tolerance go hand in hand.

But our first satisfaction in this amicable relation between accurate knowledge and free interpretation gives way to a sense of confusion when we try to establish the line that divides the two domains. Science appears to be tolerant only of such beliefs as are incapable of being confirmed or refuted by its methods. (For the unwillingness of science to pronounce in favor of conflicting theories in the absence of a crucial test is not tolerance toward different beliefs, but an abstention from belief. Nor does science merely permit or advise such suspension of judgment, but commands it, frequently in terms that do not smack of tolerance.) Religious faith, moral conscience, æsthetic appreciation have claimed freedom from compulsion, and science has frequently admitted that its methods conduct to no conclusions respecting the spiritual, the good, the beautiful. But where these claims have won the day they have taken their stand on the ground of common ignorance. Science has indeed been their useful ally in forcing ignorance to recognize itself; but beyond the confession of insufficient evidence science can not go and its so-called tolerance does not extend. Within the region which this confession affects, science, once more, can only abstain from belief: it is not freedom to believe but freedom to doubt that it champions, and in the face of doubt there is no more room for choice than in the presence of the most brutal fact. Before those who really claim the right to believe in unsupported possibilities, science can only plead its inability to grasp their meaning. "Either," it says, "your so-called beliefs are conceivably capable of confirmation or they are not. If they are, they await the event to be confirmed or refuted, as my doubts await it to be resolved. If they are not, but pose as faith in bare possibilities, they escape all chance of destruction by abandoning every vestige of content."

So the tolerance of science toward parts of experience that lie beyond its ken is an empty concession. For the only regions to which it could apply turn out to be void, or else, after all, to be remotely within its own sphere. Choice of interpretation respecting Nature vanishes as completely as caprice within Nature,—unless indeed the choice resides within the bosom of science itself. . . ?

3. *Tolerance and Subjective Choices.*—If the tolerant consciousness were willing to accept the dictum of science respecting it, the history of philosophy would end in a frank empiricism. Tolerance would call itself scientific reserve, and the only choice remaining to us would be that of acting at a risk or abstaining from acting (equally at a risk), in the face of conditions whose outcome was veiled by our ignorance. (Such reactions have no interest for us here, for the decision made in unavoidable ignorance and forced upon us by the course of events can neither be wise nor foolish, but lacks the attribute of "oughtness" we are here investigating.) But to such empiricism the claimant to the right of free opinion has an objection that recurs again and again in the history of reflection. "If," he retorts to science, "if every judgment were a bare statement of fact, then the weighing of its truth must, as you say, await the event respecting which the assertion is made. But there is an extensive class of judgments which do not pretend to be statements of fact, and whose truth rests on quite different grounds. It lies with the individual both to make these judg-

ments and to make them true. Foremost among them are just these religious, moral and æsthetic appreciations of the world. Here the individual must be the final arbiter, and tolerance is more than a confession of ignorance, it is a declaration of independence."

Such is the doctrine sometimes called "indifferentism" and we must estimate its historical significance. But because religious conviction expresses itself but vaguely (when it does not, as in the historic creeds, actually make statements of fact) and because the cry for moral liberty may not seem quite sincere (for does it not also call for social laws?), we shall confine our attention to the case of æsthetic appreciation. Here the following questions arise: Does the individual mind enjoy a freedom in ascribing beauty to the facts of Nature which is denied it in judging these facts themselves? Can the adjectives true and false be attached to the judgment of beauty at all? If so, what lies in the meaning of beauty that makes the truth of æsthetic appreciations so different in kind from that of plain statements of fact?

The first historic motives for a tolerant attitude towards appreciations of beauty are simple enough, being of the kind that express themselves in the old saw *"De gustibus."* You pronounce Mona Lisa beautiful: I call her plain—what is to be done about it? If it were a question of proportions we could appeal to the foot-rule; but that would leave the matter of the harmony of those proportions untouched. You cite Pater; I retort, "He is only a third individual." "But," you urge, "he is a judge." To which I may make one of two historic replies. The first defiant: "Who made him to be a judge over us? The individual man is the measure of beauty." The second humble: "I do not pretend to be a judge of beauty, I can only tell what I like."

According as one or the other of these replies is made, beauty is given one or the other of two meanings between which the concept has always oscillated. In the latter case it is frankly identified with a subjective liking which the judgment "this is beautiful" confesses. In the former, it is admitted that one individual may be wrong, another right in his estimate of beauty: there is such a thing as "correct taste" an "experienced judgment," and insofar the appreciation of beauty stands on a footing with the estimate of size or the description of color. We are less interested in determining which of these meanings corresponds to the place that the judgment of beauty occupies in a given culture than in asking what effect either would have upon our notion of the truth and error of æsthetic appreciations. And I think it will be seen that from neither point of view does the judgment of beauty possess peculiarities unshared by the strictest statement of fact of which science is capable.

For if, in the first place, only subjective liking is in question, there is no sense in which the avowal of such liking can be true or false unless it be the sense in which it agrees or disagrees with the facts of the case. If stress be laid on the subjectivity of these facts and their inaccessibility to any but the individual's own observation, it may equally well be pointed out that the whole structure of science is built of just such individual observations. My micrometer reading is neither more nor less accessible to you than my liking for port wine or Beethoven sonatas. And, in fact, the historic outcome of the motives that lead one to say "Man is the measure of beauty" is the doctrine that "Man is the measure of all things." If this is not wrong, yet it does not in the least interfere with the construction of a confessedly objective science; neither, then, ought it to be urged against the objectivity of beauty.

It is not, however, for any theory of beauty we are looking, but for an example of a judgment whose truth is constituted by the individual pronouncing it: if not the ascription of beauty to an object, then the avowal of liking for it; and if not that, then any judgment in which the subject seems to be sole arbiter of the truth of his own statement. So that we may at once take the highest possible ground and ask whether any expression of opinion can refer to a "last seeming" so completely subjective that the "subject" has the right to say what he will about it without risk of error.

The historic pursuit of such a type of judgment conducted the Sophists to "immediate certainty" as furnishing the final illustration. Only, it may seem odd that we should here present such certainty as a type of judgment which, all in being absolutely true, is still absolutely free. Is it not the proper historic function of this judgment to stand for that which is absolutely forced upon the subject as a bare fact of experience? I answer, the paradox goes with the paradigm, for those philosophers who with a very temerity of caution confined their estimate of truth to immediate certainty, also furnished to their successors the "horrible example" of completely wayward thinking. Nor is this an historic accident; it belongs to the nature of the "immediate" to present itself in the guise of just this contradiction: in fact it is the disorder from which it always suffers and to which it at last succumbs. For exactly that inaccessibility to more than one point of view which is supposed to shield "immediate certainty" from the danger of contradiction also robs it of the chance of confirmation. The assumption that the case can never occur again *does* make it quite indifferent what judgment is passed on it. But a little reflection will show that the only instance in which $+a = -a$ is that in which $a = o$; the only absolutely free judgment is the meaningless one. Upon Heraclitus follows Cratylus, wagging his finger in mute irony, and upon Protagoras follows Gorgias, pitifully complaining that nothing is, but that if anything were we could not know it, and if we knew it, could not tell.

Meanwhile the "subjective" and "immediate" must be given some place in experience, and they do seem to carry with them certain exemptions from outside criticism. The humility that makes no pretension to "knowledge" of beauty, but contents itself with an avowal of "liking," must yet stop somewhere. It would take it to be a poor return for its yielding disposition did the masterful critic venture to doubt the genuineness of the liking. "What impertinence," it would say, "to tell me that I do not know my own mind." And yet it may be that the critic's attitude is impertinent rather than meaningless. When one is young one feels more secure in the secret possession of a unique personal experience than when, after longer contact with life, one has formed the habit of "seeing through" others and has had the shock of being "seen through." And I am not so sure the experience of philosophy has been different from that of each individual. Gorgias found the subjective to thrive very ill on an *incomunicado* regime, and it is not unnatural that Hegel should insist on the part played by other individuals in forming the nature of the self's most intimate possessions.

However that may be, I think the dialectic of history has sufficiently emphasized the relativity of the distinction between the subjective and the objective. Insofar as a judgment lays claim to truth, insofar does it pretend to have grasped an objective reality, and insofar must it be capable of confirmation or refutation from an indefinite series of other points of view. The average of these observations (though never quite static) is the only result to which either the connoisseur of beauty or the scientific investigator can point as to the fact he is in search of. In the comparison with such an average the truth of the "subjective appreciation" appears—its freedom disappears. That which has led history to separate the truth of a judgment of beauty from that of a judgment (say) of size is the relatively large "variable error" of the former which masks the nature of the average. We have not yet found a type of judgment that does not involve a question of fact, and statements of fact are capable of a continuous treatment throughout the whole range of experience.

What then is the outcome: do we relapse into the empiricism against which the protest of tolerance is directed? That depends upon the way in which the conclusion of empiricism is stated. If, as against the tolerance we have been examining, it urges that the answer to every meaningful question must be wrung from experience and hence must involve a question of fact, I think history forces us to accept the dictum. So that if any class of judgments involves the exercise of a choice, it is because the statement of fact itself depends on choice. But if in insisting on the necessity and sufficiency of the "scientific method" empiricism views this method as excluding all choice on the part of the describer of Nature, it goes farther than we are yet justified in following it, and its conclusion must be tested by an examination of the momenta that contribute to the growth of science itself.

4. *Science and Objective Choices.*—The form that our present question must take is determined by our past admissions. We have accepted the ideal of science; the image of Nature with which our description presents us must be that of a completely determinate process, and we have agreed to admit no choice or caprice within the phenomena of Nature which would set a limit to the pursuit of this ideal. We have asked whether in some of its aspects a determinate Nature might not admit of more than one description. And we have concluded from the continuity of the concept of truth that any choice which may belong to the function of describing must be

traceable in all the ways in which this function could be exercised—in the scientific formula as well as in the ethical or æsthetic appreciation. So that our final question is this: taking scientific description as typical of all description, is there only one way, or are there more ways than one in which the scientist may present Nature as a uniquely determinate process? If more than one, and the scientific describer is constantly called upon to choose from among several, is his selection capricious or can we discover a principle by which it must be guided if his description is to be true, the Nature it portrays real?

Our first impression of the scientist is of one thrust into the midst of Nature to observe and to record. Nature flows by him as a stream of facts and it is for him to map the currents: the laws thus formulated are no less facts. *"Die Natur ist nur einmal da"* and he whose sole function is to tell what is "there" can arrive at but one result: it in no wise rests with him what this result shall be.

In this mood we think of the scientist as coming in possession of a given fact by a single observation, and as recording his observation in a categorical judgment. He measures a rod and then announces, "This rod is 1 cm. long." The laboratory observer himself, however, does not view the matter in this way. What he calls a fact is never the result of a single observation, and his record does not take on a categorical but a disjunctive form. "This rod," he will say, "is $(1 \pm \lambda)$ cm. long": *i. e.*, its length is either $(1 + \lambda)$ cm. or $(1 - \lambda)$ cm. or lies between the two. It is not merely that the scientist is cautious and repeats his observations "to make sure;" but that he is actually without means of defining the "real fact" he is in search of save in terms of an average of observations with a zero "probable error" attached. I need not point out that a zero probable error is, from the very nature of its formula, unattainable in a finite experience. Hence the probable error and the indefinite series of points of view whose variation it summarises is part of the scientist's meaning when he speaks of a "fact." The disjunction of ignorance which the probable error expresses in a quasi-categorical form is essential to any image of Nature science can evolve.

I should like to dwell on the wealth of this concept of "probable error." If I am not mistaken all the disjunctions of ignorance at which the stages of scientific progress pause could be put into this form. Were we suspended in doubt between a corpuscular and an undulatory theory of light? Then it was because the probable errors of our estimates of the velocity of light in media of different density overlapped. So, too, the probable error is the means of defining the region within which certain "neglects" that science practices are permissible. If we analyze the meaning carefully, the sense in which the "law of inertia" which seems to refer to a body "left to itself" may none the less be applied within a world in which no body could be "left to itself" will be seen to depend upon the permissible neglect of errors of detail which fall within a "probable error" of result—an error whose magnitude is independently fixed.

I mention these matters for two reasons. First, because since science must always present us with disjunctions, it seems always to be leaving us an alternative which makes a choice not only permissible but imperative. And some recent philosophers have held that the psychological factors determining the choice of an individual scientist at such junctures may have a permanent influence on "the result."[1] Second, because other philosophers have contended that since such axioms as Newton's "law of inertia" cannot be literally illustrated in Nature, therefore science "abstracts" from Nature and gives us, instead of a true image, an "ideal construction" on which it would be unsafe to form our *Weltanschauung*.[2] But when we see that all the disjunctions with which science presents us are really of the nature of that "probable error" which must attach to any statement of fact, does it not seem that we

[1] James, *Will to Believe*.
[2] Ward, *Naturalism and Agnosticism*.

have already taken account of these "psychological factors"? Are they not among the very causes which lead to variation between observers and of which the "probable error" gives a summary statement? They no doubt play their part in the drama of science, but they belong in the chorus. For the rest, I am here only stating in another form the view already accepted that the disjunction of ignorance is no ground for a play of choice, but only for a wavering of doubt.[1] And as to the "abstractions" of science, I can only find suggestion of them in the careless abbreviations of the scientist and in the unfair interpretations of the critic. Science may be an "ideal construction" but its ideals do not involve the neglect of facts.

I must leave this subject of the "probable error" which has helped us to pass beyond the impression that a statement of fact is the categorical utterance of an individual observation and enabled us first to detect its *disjunctive* character, then to trace in the result the contributions of a society of observers. Even now we have not exhausted the meaning which a simple statement of fact has for the scientific observer. If the "probable error" is of the nature of a disjunction, so the concept of the "constant error" points to a *condition* involved in a statement of fact. "This rod is indeed $(1 \pm \lambda)$ cm. long, but only *if*

[1] This view was somewhat modified later. *Vid.* p. 285 sqq. ''The Mathematician and His Luck.''

the temperature be t degrees, the stress f dynes, etc." Omit these conditions and the statement is meaningless: misrepresent them and, however faithfully it may record observations actually made, it is false: it is affected by a "constant error."

From this it would follow that the very simplest statement exact science can make about Nature—the one from which all its generalizations start, the record of an individual fact—must take on a *hypothetical* form. Yet it would seem that this much of the naïve attitude towards science from which we started must remain true to the end; namely, that the account of Nature which interests us most must finally be expressed in categorical (or quasi-categorical) judgments. We want to know what has happened and most of all what will happen, and cannot remain eternally satisfied with the knowledge that if a should come about then we must look out for b. And since science undertakes to satisfy us on this score, since it does make categorical predictions, the question naturally arises: What has become of the conditional clauses?

The answer is not far to seek. Neglect such conditions as cling to every statement of fact science cannot without loss of meaning: absorb them in the categorical judgment itself it can and does. And that by a very simple device: the setting up by convention of so-called "standard conditions." Now as

CHOICE AND NATURE

regards these conventions there are several things to be noticed. First, they are said to be "arbitrary," which does not mean that they are unmotived and capricious, but only that they result from a choice. Second, this choice is social, not individual, and constitutes the "universe of discourse" within which the individual judgment is meaningful and true. Third, this choice selects from among several alternative accounts of Nature, each of which presents Nature as a thoroughly determinate process. Finally, no categorical account of Nature, *i. e.*, no image of Nature "in the concrete," can be given which does not embody a series of such choices.

But in spite of the fact that the Nature we point to with hope or with fear is always a Nature described, it is generally felt that there is a difference between Nature-in-itself and the description we give of it. However completely the choices we have mentioned may be embodied in the "universe of discourse" yet this can never be identified with *the* Universe: the conventions are purely "nominal." *"Il y a le nom et la chose,"* says Montaigne, *"le nom ce n'est pas une partie de la chose, ni de la substance: c'est une pièce étrangère jointe à la chose, et hors d'elle."* [1]

Now it is quite true that the choices and conventions of which we have spoken are in the nature of

[1] Montaigne's *Essai*, "De la gloire."

definitions. In the example of length we were merely watching the growth of the definition of length to meet the needs of a more refined description. So that we may pass at once to the general question of the definition or, let us say, of classification. Then it will be seen that the motives which inspire the preceding paragraph are those that lead Kant to treat definitions as analytic judgments and, being such, as essentially different from any other *a priori* factors of knowledge which may really help to "constitute" experience as we know it.

There is no doubt that this insistence upon the triviality of definition and classification in our system of knowledge strikes a sympathetic chord in the common understanding,—one which responds in terms of such saws as "Soft words butter no parsnips" or the poet's line, "A rose by any other name would smell as sweet." At the same time we must not forget that the very opposite of view has received historic expression: *e. g.*, in the mot *"La science est une langue bien faite."* Now, as has been said in the introductory paragraph, the whole history of philosophy is a dialectic growing out of such antitheses as the one before us. And generally we have learned that the contrast arises from a breach of continuity to re-establish which is to grasp the truth of the situation.

Just so here: it is no doubt always possible

to distinguish between the facts of Nature and a classification to which they are subjected. If it were not for the indifference of such facts to the various ways in which they could be classified, the problem of arrangement would not present that element of choice which we have insisted upon. But to be indifferent toward certain alternative classifications is not to be independent of all classification, and it must always be equally possible to show that these facts presented in Nature are themselves the resultants of finished classification: if they were not they could not be "presented." Those whose attention is attracted by the factual aspect of Nature fly to one limit: "we do not really know Nature until we get at the 'solid' facts, untainted by arbitrary arrangement and eternally indifferent to the way in which we classify them." Those who recognize the important part that classification plays in the final image of Nature rush to the other extreme: "knowledge is nothing but the game of arrangement."

But if there is one thing the dialectic of history seems to have established more firmly than another it is that, not at the "limits," but in the continuous series which defines them, lies the truth. Whatever is required to account for the way in which one of its stages follows on another is essential to the nature of experience. And since at any stage of our growing knowledge at which we try to tell what Nature is, the describer is presented with a choice, and since no stage can be found which does not embody past choices, I take it that this series of choices is involved in anything we do or can mean by Nature.

5. *The Choices of Science and Their Truth.*—
It is not well that a philosopher should be let off with a generality. If he has really caught a fragment of the truth, let him show where it fits into the scheme of experience. I shall try to do this with respect to the choices of science by showing where in the history of science such choices have been exercised, and how they have gradually moulded the meaning we now attach to the term "Nature." But to illustrate systematically would be to write a history of science, for we have said that such choices must be exercised continually and work gradual transformations. The best that can be done in brief space is to look for the most striking instances, and to lay them before the reader with little comment. In each case, too, we may answer a question raised at the beginning of our search into scientific method by pointing out that these choices have not been exercised capriciously, but according to a given principle. Science has regarded one alternative as preferable to another and has treated the ground of preference as a ground of truth. And when we have finished I think we shall see the exercise of such choices to be the only factor in experience that has any claim to

be called *a priori:* whether or not we retain for them the term analytic, we shall at least have grasped all the motives that have led to the doctrine of *a priori* synthetic judgments, once we have seized on the Nature-making power of such choices.

Since we have stated the function of choice to be exercised in the business of classification, we naturally turn for our first illustration to the science in which the problem of classification has received the greatest recognition. The day is not long past when the main question of biology was that of "true orders." The biologist of this time felt that it had a meaning to ask whether a given scheme of classification were true or false. "I will not give my reasons," writes Linnæus, "for the distribution of the natural orders which I have published. You or some other person after twenty or fifty years will discover them and *see that I was right.*" [1] It is the language of the "realist" that looks for classes *in re*—a language we still speak when we distinguish between "artificial" and "natural" systems of classification. And yet it is clear that there are many consistent classifications to which the facts presented to Linnæus were susceptible.

The period that witnessed this struggle after "true orders" culminated in the genetic classification of evolutionist biology. Is this a truer arrangement

[1] Romanes, *Darwin and after Darwin*, Vol. 1, p. 26.

than any other consistent grouping that could be devised? I only point out here that the way in which a classification is made determines the next question the scientist asks. The question may then be "put to Nature" and receive an empirical solution; but it cannot be answered until it is asked. Now the peculiarity of the genetic classification was that it led to a form of question which did not apply to biology alone. Other principles of division would have been as consistent with the facts *given* to them, but respecting the facts *resulting* from them we could not have asked: "Are they the results of development?" The search for the "mechanical factors" of evolution would never have troubled us, nor engaged us with its broad promise of unified sciences. And yet it is the insight into just these analogies which, as the patient Kepler said, leads us into the arcana of Nature. When we ask what Nature *is*, it is in terms of such insights we are answered. It is in this sense that a classification can be "true to Nature": it is in this sense that classes can be said to exist *in* Nature. One is all the more a realist for being idealist enough to see in Nature the embodiment of choices.

Let us turn to another instance and another science. We shall see the "analytic" aspect of choice gradually slipping away; for in the case we now take up historic science did not even notice that its problem had an analytic side, but supposed itself to be facing a bare question of fact. I suppose most will remember to have been taught that modern astronomy dates from Copernicus's "discovery" that the earth revolves around the sun and not *vice versa*. Huxley speaks of the old "geocentric system of astronomy with its eccentrics and epicycles" as "an hypothesis utterly at variance with fact."[1] And it is common enough to hear the Church of the period upbraided for flying in the face of facts.

Yet when one's attention is called to it, I fancy no one will fail to justify Mach's contention that the Copernican change of standpoint was only a change of standpoint and raised no question of fact.[2] The paths of the planets are necessarily describable with respect either to the sun or to the earth as origin. The question of the origin of co-ordinates is a question of interpretation, and it is decided in favor of relative simplicity. The "truth" which this advantage seemed to impart to the Copernican point of view appeared to Huxley to have the same cogency to force acceptance as has a fact to compel belief. Hence he regarded the question of origin, not only as one capable of a right and wrong answer, but actually as a question of fact.

I might recount the sequel to this historic incident,

[1] *Progress of Science.*
[2] *Mechanics in Its Development*, p. 232.

CHOICE AND NATURE

how the change of origin effected by Copernicus made Kepler's questions possible; how the resulting laws made it posible for Newton to ask the same question of the moon that Galileo asked of falling bodies and Huygens of a ball swung on a string; how these general views of motion suggested the query: is the whole system of visible motions a self-repeating cycle?—and how, on the assumption (afterwards empirically verified) that it is not, the concept of motion is included by Kant and Laplace under that of growth: until at last our image of Nature includes an evolution of mechanical processes, as well as the mechanical processes of evolution. Each stage would be seen to depend upon certain choices of arrangement, and a history of science written with these in view would be the realization of Hankel's ideal: *"Die Geschichte einer Wissenschaft kann selbst Wissenschaft werden."* [1]

But it is better to have exhausted the significance of a few illustrations than to have squandered many. I have been laying emphasis on the *a priori* part

[1] *Gesch. d. Math.* I should like to have included among these illustrations the much disputed problem of geometrical axioms. For I think the question as to what experiment proves respecting the truth and the error of these axioms depends upon what we let it prove. If they are *a priori* they are so by command, and it is for this reason aand not because of a happy chance, that the true axioms are the simplest. The matter, however, proved too subtle to be condensed into a paragraph. If the reader is intrested in this point of view I may refer him, as to the treatment most closely in sympathy with it, to Poincairé (*Rev. de Mét. et de Mor.* 1895, 631; 1899, 251; *Monist*, 1898, 1.).

211

of our thinking, and the reader may have felt that justice has not been done to the *a posteriori*. Let us put the feeling into a question. The results of Kepler and Newton led to the discovery of a new planet whose behavior was in accordance with their predictions. But suppose accident were to lead to the discovery of another which did not conform (say) to Kepler's laws, should we not reject those laws? Are we not then dealing with descriptions of Nature whose truth reduces to an agreement with the facts?

That every judgment capable of truth or error *involves* a question of fact I not only admit but have been at some pains to defend: that it *reduces* to a question of fact I cannot see. No doubt we should reject a scientific law in the face of an exception; but the form in which we should express our new knowledge is not uniquely determined. Our first step is to replace a universal affirmative proposition with an exceptive; but it is not our last. And why? The determinateness of our image of Nature is not interfered with by stating a law and its exception. "All planets except X obey a certain law and X obeys another:" the space distribution of planets at a given instant of time is determinate enough. What we have lost is the simplicity of our formula, and it is because we choose that our description of Nature shall be simple, that we reject a formula which permits of exception as not representing a law of Nature. We assume that the description of this determinate flow of facts we call the course of Nature is capable of complete expression in universal judgments. What right have we to proceed on such an assumption? Is it that we detect on the part of facts an eagerness to oblige? They are not noted for such complaisance: philosophers have even been known to call them "brutal." Is it not rather because we have the remaking of the facts within our power? And this by reconsidering an old choice of classification: in the resistance that facts offer to our desires is always to be detected the opposition of our old choices to our present needs. It is for this reason that the search for a universal formula for Nature is always bound to succeed.

For example, Newton's law of universal gravitation is actually subject to many exceptions. Not every body of matter attracts every other with a force proportionate directly to the product of the masses and inversely to the square of the distance between their centres of gravity. This is only true in case the bodies are without electric charges, do not possess magnetic poles and have other negative properties. So far science has been content to state our physical laws in terms of exceptions, and instead of a single formula for Nature we have several.

CHOICE AND NATURE

The image of a Nature resulting is determinate enough save for "probable errors." But modern analytical mechanics is not satisfied with mere determinateness: it demands simplicity. Consequently we find it throwing the mass of phenomena into a single formula—the generalized Hamiltonian principle or the generalized Lagrangian equations.[1] It is not pretended that this is more than a "formal" transformation of *all* the formulæ of physics, for it does not really reduce the number of "dimensions" (since the same term in the formula has different though analogous meanings within different classes of phenomena) and it introduces no new determinateness. For that reason such transformations must always be possible. But what is the next step? By treating the system of bodies *as though* it included concealed motions we manage (perhaps after the manner of Hertz) to express the different determining properties of the bodies in terms of the velocities of these motions. Now we have really reduced the number of dimensions to mass, space and time, but we have not reduced the indeterminateness due to "probable errors": we have introduced no new observation of facts. And what does this hypothetical *"as though"* mean? For a system to *have* a certain constitution, and for a

[1] The most satisfactory account of this process appears to me to be that given by Helmholtz, *Vorlesungen über die Theoretische Physik*, Vol. I, p. 2.

214

system to behave *as though it had* a certain constitution, mean the same thing: the moon behaves as though it had another side. All that we have done is to introduce a new classification which has the conditional flavor of all classifications, a flavor that only fades away as the classification ceases to be new. We no longer state our law in terms of "all bodies" in Newton's sense, adding exceptions that apply to different *kinds* of bodies; we state our formula in terms of mass, space and time. The kinds of bodies and motions are characterized by the different degrees in which these dimensions belong to them, and Newton's view of the situation appears as a special case, along with its exceptions, the other special cases. Can the facts obstruct such progress? I think not: a classification that possesses maximum simplicity must always be possible, and if at any stage new observations lead to exceptions, these do not *force* a rejection of old choices, but they *invite* it. "The order and uniformity of the phenomena we call Nature, we ourselves introduce into them, and we had never been able to find it there had we not first put it there."[1] Thus did Kant from a somewhat different point of view express much the same thought.

6. *Nature, Choice and Will.*—It would seem, then, that when we wonder at the order and sim-

[1] *Kr. d. r. Vernunft,* A p. 125 (Abridged).

plicity of Nature, we wonder at our own handiwork as Nature-builders—"The heavens declare the glory of Kepler and Newton." And if, with Omar, we find the scheme of things "sorry," can we not "shatter it to bits and then remold it nearer to the heart's desire"? We not only can do so, but constantly are doing so—it is the function of science. Only, the "heart's desire" must not be unprincipled. In the historical illustrations we have seen that the choice exercised by the describer is regarded as true only insofar as it abides by a certain principle, which we might variously call the principle of maximum simplicity, economy or unity. It remains to be shown *why* this choice should be regarded as true.

In the first place it will be recognized that the demand for maximum unity expresses a strong intellectual need. But it is not the only need of our nature, it is not shared by every one,—as witnesses the attitude of the Church toward Copernicus. And even supposing it the predominant need, why should it not determine the utility rather than the truth of our description of Nature?

We have seen that the choices which play a part in the constitution of Nature are exercised in the function of classification. Now there is only one sense in which we commonly apply the term error to a classification,—it is that which we illustrated in the case of "constant error," that which permits us to speak of a wrong definition. Error in this sense must always involve the contrast between an individual and a social choice. If then we have a right to gratify any need of our being in exercising the choices we have been considering, it must be because the need is universal,—it is a principle that expresses a universal will. But there are many needs whose wide distribution throughout society we can discover by observation. If the criterion of universality is to be empirical, there is no reason for satisfying the intellectual rather than the æsthetic or "spiritual" needs,—and this is the position taken by some modern writers.[1]

But all through our study we have seen that the will which is reflected in a true image of Nature is not expressed in a mere *consensus gentium*. We justify Copernicus although he was a minority of one: we condemn the Church that stood for the voice of the people and the voice of God. The will to which Copernicus appealed was broader than his age,—and the will we are now in search of must be thought *sub specie æternitatis*.

The search for the absolutely universal will is one that has been attempted before,—at least the method of search has been defined. For if we are not to stop at an empirical generality but to find the

[1] James, *op. cit.*

principle of choice that would be exercised by all describers in the face of all possible experience, it is evident that we seek the principle without which no description, no experience and, consequently, no Nature is possible. We are faced with the old problem of deduction as it appeared to Kant. Our demand for universal will is not a little like his motive for seeking "categories," and we may rest satisfied with expanding Kant's method to fit our needs.

The conclusion of Kant's deduction is that the trait of experience without which there could be no experience, and yet which does not belong to an aggregate of bare facts, is unity; and in this unity is reflected the activity of a describing consciousness. We have arrived at the same conclusion in our own way. But Kant's attitude toward experience leaves it, in several respects, static. Its movement is a flow of facts: the "forms" into which these facts fit are ready-made categories. As a result the forms of thought "constitute" experience in giving to it its unity; but the evolution of unity, the struggle after maximum unity, falls under merely "regulative principles." Thus a permanent separation between *truth* and the *value* of description is allowed.

It may be said, I think, that the outcome of post-Kantian thought is a transition from a static to a dynamic attitude toward experience. Its "flow" is no longer a mere flow of facts, but an evolution of interpretations. It is such evolution that Hegel is constantly dwelling upon (*die Bewegung*). From this point of view, it is not the unity of our thought but our thought's struggle after maximum unity that constitutes experience what it is. It is this desire for maximum unity that we struggle to satisfy and the gratification of which constitutes the truth of an interpretation. The desire is, of course, a fact of our experience, but it is to be distinguished from other empirical needs in that the right to gratify it is to be deduced from the meaning of experience itself, within which it is the absolutely universal principle of choice. It is this that makes maximum unity a true not merely a useful, a constitutive not merely a regulative principle. I need not point out that all our illustrations have been so many scenes from the drama of human thought struggling after maximum unity in the building of the world of Nature.

But now if the choices that are not determined by fact are determined by the principle of maximum unity whose claim to truth depends upon its necessity to the very meaning of experience, has not individual liberty to satisfy individual need completely disappeared? And if so, what has become of the illustrations cited in this very paper in which the individual,—yes, the larger part of society,—

rejected this universal principle? The Church opposed the astronomical scheme of Copernicus, and yet the Church not only meant something by its attitude but still continues to live and to function.

It would be interesting to show the difference between the sense in which the "unity of apperception" was felt by Kant to be a universal and necessary condition of experience, and that in which maximum unity represents to us the will of a universal society. But I must confine myself to an example which will tend to show the kind of liberty an individual may possess to resist a law without which the society of which he is a part and to which he owes his own nature could not exist. I take the specialized type of experience we call "life." Life is what it is because the living being is essentially a struggling being. From this it does not follow that every living being enters consciously into the struggle. There are the fortunate ones who toil not neither do they spin, and yet continue to live. To them struggle may seem a mere accident of life and not its essence. But we must see that they could not thus live were they not part of a society which is a struggling society and heirs to the ages that were ages of conflict. They are made in the image of the surviving fittest, and idle as they may wish to be they cannot give up all the functions made necessary by the struggle and continue to live. So far

CHOICE AND NATURE

as they do give up the struggle, they do *give up*, *i. e.*, the very definition of their apathy is couched in terms of the strife they strive to shun,—and in shunning, recognize.

So with experience as a whole: the individual has a certain liberty to decide untruly. Whether from indifference (the apathy of surrender), or from pride (the self-will of a romantic genius that a Nietzsche expresses), or from prejudice (the bigotry of the Church in the preceding example), history is full of instances of the denial of the will to experience. But this denial carried to the limit means extinction, and carried part way means partial stagnation: experience may die by inches. In all cases its essential characteristic is denial or revolt, and that recognizes the nature of the law against which it revolts. It need scarcely be remarked that this individual may be a very large group. The human race may for ages be lethargic. But the dark ages contain the germ of an *Aufklärung* and moreover are not themselves completely without light.

From all this the relation of Nature to the individual desire follows of itself. We have represented the individual as faced with a group of facts; but not of bare facts, for insofar as these have even enough meaning to be pointed out as facts they bear the traces of description with all that this implies of past choices. So that at no stage is he presented with a situation so purely factual that it cannot be altered by re-interpretation. Observation has, of course, an important place in his life; but his experience is not increased by bare additions. The real importance of observation is to serve as the stimulus to new interpretations. These interpretations we have seen were indeterminate save for a principle of choice not yielded by the facts themselves. Yet this choice is not the individual's own; but that of the society to which he belongs. Nor is this society just of his day and generation, for that is only a larger individual, but the universal society to contradict whose will is to destroy the meaning of experience. Such a will dictates a principle of choice gratifying a desire an individual may well enough possess. Insofar, then, as the individual desires what all must desire if they would have experience, Nature as embodying our interpretations must yield him satisfaction. But insofar as the desire is purely individual, Nature offers no guarantee that it shall be gratified.

As the type of universal desire we have taken maximum unity—a rather cold, intellectual one, it may seem. It would be interesting, did space permit, to consider the question "Are not the demands for the goodness and beauty of our world involved in this?" It may be that the concepts of unity, goodness and beauty are more closely allied than their frequently contradictory expressions would lead us to suspect: history is full of attempts to identify them. The old scholastic formula *"Quodlibet ens est unum, et verum et bonum"* may be profoundly true. For the present, however, I must leave this question untouched.[1]

[1] *Cf.* "Modern Thinkers," the discussion of "progress."

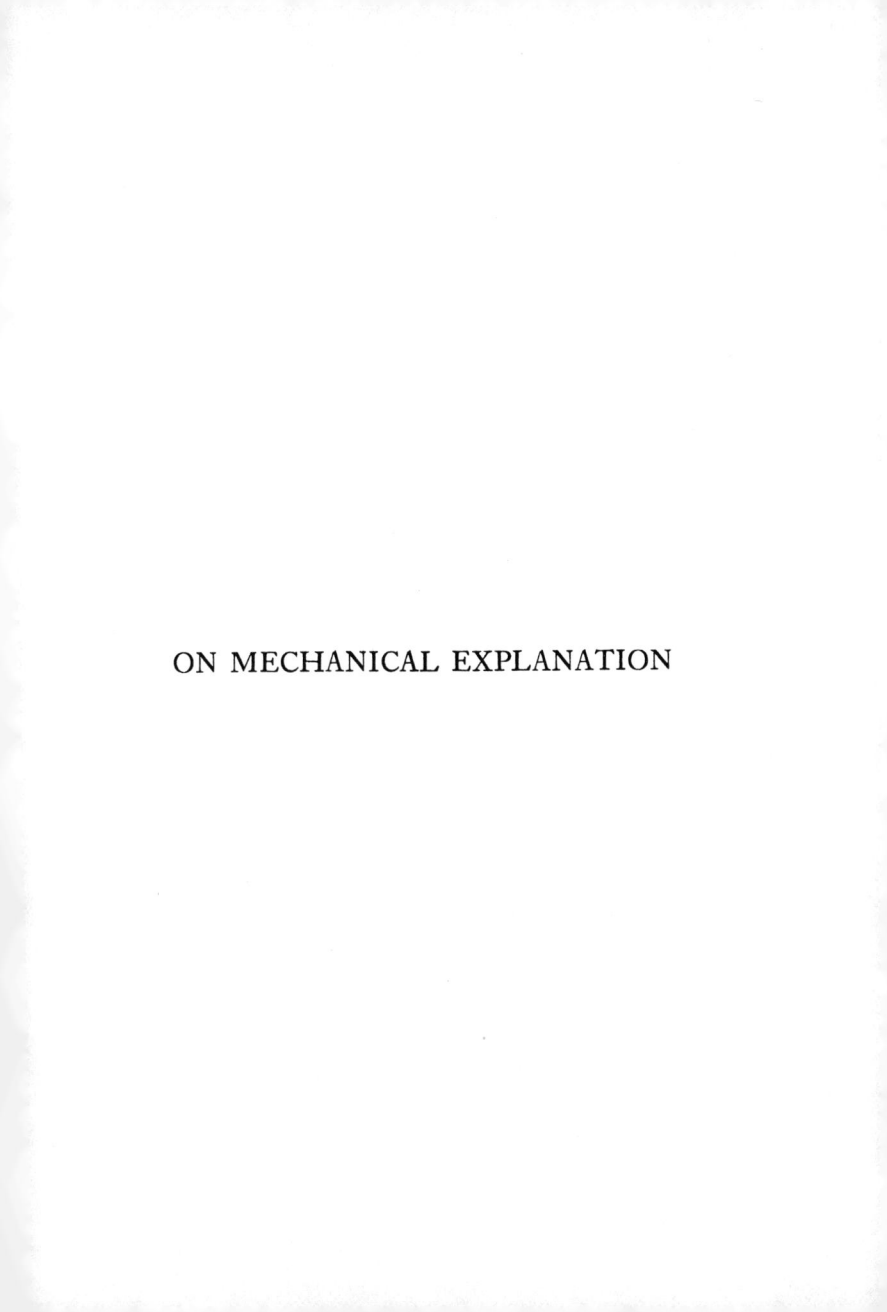

ON MECHANICAL EXPLANATION

XI.

ON MECHANICAL EXPLANATION

I. *On the Definition of the Mechanical Ideal.*—
In philosophy and in science we are frequently called upon to face a certain hypothesis,—the hypothesis, namely, that all the phenomena of the world in which we live are susceptible of a mechanical explanation. In discussing method we are in the habit of referring to this point of view as the "mechanical ideal." Now we all feel that in a way we understand what is meant by the mechanical ideal, whether or not we are willing to entertain it, and yet it must be admitted that the literature of philosophy is much richer in instances of an instinctive application of this ideal than in examples of a serious effort to define its meaning. We feel no little confidence in our right to pronounce certain methods of explanation inharmonious with the ideal, but such exclusions still leave us in considerable doubt respecting the inclusion of the term.

For example, it would probably be admitted by all that a biologist who denied the possibility of finding among the physico-chemical conditions of an organism and its environment at any moment the determinants of any change in the organism at that moment, would definitely have rejected the mechanical ideal. But, on the other hand, would the adoption of a physio-chemical theory of organic change be equivalent to the acceptance of the ideal? At least, we can understand the eagerness of an Ostwald to replace the vague concept of "chemical affinity" with a picture whose details are wholly physical of the processes involved in neutralization, solution, and so forth. This sympathy may be taken as the expression of an instinctive feeling that the phenomena of chemistry themselves are in need of a mechanical explanation. A like satisfaction attends every successful effort to reproduce certain physical phenomena (for example, those of heat) in terms of concealed mass-motions. In short, a type of explanation which at one stage of our progress and with a view to certain exclusions we may advance as mechanical, will itself appear at another stage to be in need of mechanical explanation. It would thus seem that the use of the concept in question is subject to that vacillation which makes definition of it at once difficult and imperative.

To begin with, the most natural suggestion, and the one most closely in accord with historical development, would view our ideal as arranging the sciences in a "tree" of subsumptions of such nature that we might regard each science as capable of reduction to the one next below it; until at last we arrived at a radical science to which all the others might be reduced. The adjective "mechanical" attached to our ideal would then indicate that this fundamental science was none other than the science of mechanics. Indeed, it has seldom occurred to the scientist that there could be any sense in which the phenomena of mechanics themselves were in need of further explanation. If this suggestion be adopted, our task of defining the mechanical ideal will be accomplished when we have given a definition of mechanics and an explanation of the sense in which one science is capable of reduction to another. Such an insight into the meaning of the term having been obtained, we may proceed to examine the grounds which could be urged for the acceptance of the ideal as a guide to our speculation.

In defining the science of mechanics, it is necessary that our method should make use of such differentiæ as are of general application. The problem of the classification of the sciences is very far from having reached solution, but as a contribution to it I may suggest that the characteristics which best distinguish a science are those which, in technical language, are termed the "dimensions" of the science. The concept of the dimensions of a science, although of familiar application, is not quite easy to define; that is, it is difficult to bring it under the concept of dimensions in general. For our present purpose, it will be sufficient to illustrate the meaning of dimensions and to show in what sense they may be used to differentiate the sciences.

As a particularly simple case, let us consider the dimensions of a system of bodies to which we might give the name of a Laplacian system. Such a system would be defined in terms of the familiar image once offered by Laplace; that is, it would be a system such that, if we knew the masses, the space distribution, and the velocities at all points at any given moment, we should be able to calculate the masses, the space distribution, and the velocities at all points for any other moment. The formula by which such a calculation would be made might be called the axiom of the science dealing with such systems. It is evident that there are four independent observations which must be made at every point in this system, and which must be substituted in its formula, before any determinate problem is presented to us. These four independent observations are mass, length, time, and velocity; and the use to which we put them might suggest an analogy with the way in which we use independent coördinates to determine the position of an element in any dimensional manifold. The concept of the dimensions of our science, however, differs slightly from this, in that we consider, not the independent data, but the independent kinds of measurement involved. Thus velocity, being a ratio of length and time, is not regarded as a dimension in the sense now contemplated, but implicitly contains the dimensions of length and time; so that in the end the dimensions of a science dealing with Laplacian systems would be mass, length, and time.

With the concept of a dimension now clear, we may proceed to define mechanics as the science whose dimensions are mass, length, and time. We shall, of course, not be understood to identify mechanics with the science of the Laplacian systems in the sense of the preceding illustration; for, while such a science would certainly be mechanical, the converse is not implied, that mechanics is the science of Laplacian systems. If, in fact, we were to compare this definition with the contents of an ordinary textbook of mechanics, we should see that our definition was both broader and narrower than that which is implied in the subjects there treated of. It is broader, for the reason that it would include such widely divergent systems of mechanics as those based on the theory of rigid connections, on the one hand, and those based on the theory of action at a distance, on the other. It is narrower in that it would exclude certain problems which are generally handled in text-books on mechanics and yet which we cannot regard as properly mechanical,— for example, the problems of impact. For evidently no knowledge of the masses, space distribution, and length-and-time quotients, would inform us whether two colliding bodies would behave as elastic or as inelastic bodies. Without this knowledge, however, the problem of impact is indeterminate. The knowledge itself can only be conveyed in terms of a coefficient of elasticity, for the present to be regarded as a new dimension. Our breadth, however, is evidently proper to a definition designed to include the common feature of all schools of mechanics, without taking sides on questions of detail. Our narrowness succeeds in relegating to the domain of general physics phenomena recognized as lacking a purely mechanical solution.

Mechanics, then, is the science whose dimensions are mass, length, and time; it remains to be seen what is meant, when we speak of reducing other sciences to mechanics. Our method of offering such an explanation must depend upon the acceptance of our suggestion that the various sciences may be differentiated in terms of their dimensions. This suggestion requires some defense. It will be seen at once that it is neatly applicable to the definition of certain recognized branches of physics. For example, thermodynamics would involve the additional dimension *temperature;* electrostatics and electrodynamics, the additional dimension *quantity of electricity;* magnetism, the dimension *strength of pole.* But it will not at once be evident that there is any sense in which we could define chemistry in terms of a specific dimension or group of dimensions, and a like difficulty would pertain to the definition of biology, psychology, sociology, etc.

As for chemistry, we must distinguish between its condition in the past, in which it presented a series of more or less general observations refusing to be united in any single formula, and a tendency towards systematization which characterizes its present. There are, it would seem, two main problems of chemistry: (1) to deduce the properties of a compound from the properties of the elements entering into it; (2) to develop a formula by which the various properties of elements may be expressed as functions of one of their number, which may then be taken as defining the element.

In connection with the first of these problems, Ostwald has divided the properties of compounds into the "additive," the "constitutive," and the "colligative." The "additive" properties of a compound are the simple sum of the properties of the elements combined: thus the molecular mass is the sum of the atomic masses. The "constitutive" properties are those which depend not only on the elements combined, but upon a factor which is usually called the "arrangement" of these elements. The "colligative," finally, depend wholly upon the arrangement of the elements. If, now, as Ostwald suspects, it should be found that the "constitutive" and "colligative" properties are ultimately reducible to the "additive," or if the factor which is termed "arrangement" may be conceived to depend on the space-distribution,—or space-order, let us say,—the whole problem of the properties of compounds presents no dimension which does not belong to the elements themselves. If, on the other hand, the reduction of "constitutive" and "colligative" properties to "additive" cannot be effected, or if the factor of "arrangement" cannot be conceived in spatial terms, the science of chemical compounds must possess a specific dimension of its own.

Again, the immediate result of the attempt to express all the properties of elements in terms of one of their number taken to be characteristic, is illustrated in the formulation of the periodic law. Imperfect as this scheme is recognized to be, it was still possible for Mendelyeff to predict the properties of an element as yet unobserved from the assumption of its atomic mass, and to find his prediction confirmed by later observation. The possession of such a formula as the periodic law suggests would have a tendency to make atomic mass the dimension of chemistry.

May we not, therefore, say that insofar as chemistry succeeds in being a single science rather than tables of collated observations, that single science is definable by a specific dimension? And conversely, in so far as we are unable to assign any dimension to chemistry, does not the application of a single name to entirely independent observations depend rather upon an association of ideas, upon accidental similarity of method, than upon any right to regard that name as capable of a unique definition?

As to the other sciences mentioned, biology, psychology, sociology, etc., it is clear that they are interested in laws applicable to complex wholes. The terms in which these laws are stated are in general not applicable to the parts of which the wholes are composed. The question, then, as to whether these sciences are definable in terms of specific dimensions, is not identical with the question as to whether they are definable at all. If, for example, it were admitted that the phenomena of organic life could not be explained in terms of the physical and chemical constituents of an organism, it might be possible that a study of biology would lead to the discovery of a dimension which the physics and chemistry alluded to had not included. In this sense it has been suggested that "vital force" might be regarded as a property related, say, to magnetic force as magnetic force is related to gravitation. To appeal to such a force would be to attempt to give biology a specific dimension. But if no such appeal is made, and if the biologist admits the laws of the totals with which he is dealing to be quite consistent with the physico-chemical laws of the parts which compose them, the science does not in the least cease to be definable, but it ceases to be an independent science. Its definition must not be sought in the mechanics of the totals or groups it deals with. For this reason I am in the habit of referring to a science thus defined as a "superimposed" science. It will be seen, then, that the differentiation of the sciences in terms of their dimensions is a differentiation which is only meaningful in case these sciences are independent; and conversely, to define a science as a "superimposed" science is to admit that it possesses no specific dimensions. For the rest, we are not interested in the question as to whether biology, psychology, and sociology are really "superimposed" sciences or not.

Enough has perhaps been said to make it clear in what sense our suggestion that sciences may be differentiated in terms of their dimensions is applicable throughout the whole range of independent sciences. The advantage of this method of differentiation is that it yields us immediately the statement for which we have been in search, of the meaning of reduction. We may now say in general that *any science* x, *dimensions* abcd, *is reducible to any science* y, *dimensions* abc, *when it may be shown in any manner that the term* d *is expressible as a function of* abc. For example, let x be the science of thermodynamics, whose dimensions are mass, length, time, and temperature; and let y be the science of mechanics. The reduction of thermodynamics to mechanics is effected when we show that temperature is a function of mass, length, and time, or of any pair of these three terms. This reduction is exactly the one ostensibly effected by the mechanical theory of heat, in which it has been made to appear that temperature is a function of the velocity of certain concealed mass-motions. It would be easy to find in the physical speculations of our day other reductions of an exactly similar nature. Such a reduction having been made, the reduced science loses its independence with its specific dimension, and if retained in our thinking at all, must be treated as "superimposed" science.

Thus we obtain, as the most general statement of the traditional mechanical ideal, the hypothesis that *mass, length, and time, are the dimensions of natural science.*

II. *On the Possibility of the Mechanical Ideal.*—Having defined the mechanical ideal in a way enjoying at least the advantage of displaying its own motives, we are now in a position to consider the arguments apt to be advanced for its acceptance or its rejection. We may at once lay aside as irrelevant all reference to our present accomplishment in the premises. It is obvious that we are indefinitely remote from the realization of the ideal as it has been defined; it is no less plain that many steps of modern progress might readily be looked upon as conducting us toward such a goal. But if no discussion of this problem save the *a posteriori* is possible, our only business for the present is to possess our souls in patience and to await the results of experimental science. As an historical fact, however, there have been advanced reasons purporting to be *a priori* for supposing the attainment of our end to be impossible, and other reasons laying no less claim to an *a priori* character for expecting with confidence its ultimate realization. It is to a consideration of these *a priori* grounds for acceptance or rejection that we now turn. In the present paper I shall confine myself to the arguments *contra*, reserving for a future occasion the discussion of the arguments *pro*.[1]

That a mechanical image of nature can never be constructed has been urged on one of two grounds, —either on the ground that the image is self-contradictory and so meaningless, or on the ground that it is essentially untrue to nature. The former objection goes back to Parmenides and Zeno; it has never lacked representatives. The latter has been insisted upon most obstinately by those who have been impressed with the multitude of purposeful processes in nature, and who cannot convince themselves that nature could be described or its happenings predicted without making use of expressions having reference to ends; but such reference, they feel, implies other laws than those enabling us to define a mechanical system.

Such objections to the meaningfulness of the mechanical image as turn on the difficulties in defining

[1] [The ''mechanical ideal'' just defined has been referred to as *the traditional*. Had I undertaken to discuss the fate of an *ultimate* ideal that might go by the same name, I must have been careful to insist on the indifference of *this* mechanical ideal to the name and kind of the dimensions to which it strove to reduce its description of nature. Its interest centered in the *number* of dimensions exact science must use, it struggles to diminish this number in the way set forth, unconcerned as to what its image of nature reduces *to*. But as the ''traditional'' meaning amply arms the two mechanical ideals against such objections as would be sure to be urged against both, the discussion best accomplished its purpose by stopping short of ''ultimate'' things. (Appended.)].

mass, length, time, and their combinations, cannot be detailed in this connection; we should find ourselves involved in some of the most perplexing chapters of metaphysics. Yet we are not prevented from taking at once a certain attitude toward this class of objections. To any one who thinks that he has discovered contradictions or insufficiencies in the definitions ordinarily offered in the field of geometry, kinematics, and mechanics, we can only reply that it would be surprising if such imperfecions were not to be found. The history of the search for definitions from Socrates to the present time makes nothing plainer than that the terms we use most instinctively are the ones whose meaning it is most difficult to set forth. But on the whole we make progress. The particular inadequacy of mass, as defined by Newton, is not to be found in Mach's definition. Hertz, while admitting this, is still dissatisfied with the accomplishment of Mach; and if Hertz be not justified, nothing is more likely than that another critic will be. There is every reason to hope, however, that since the modern systematist has detected and removed the imperfections of Newton, the future critic will be able to detect and to remove what flaws may be latent in our current system. The history of the concept of mass is repeated in that of the other dimensions. No one who is acquainted with the problem of framing the axioms of geometry and kinematics is going to stake much on the perfection of any system that has yet been advanced; but neither can one find any ancient difficulty which from Euclid to Hilbert and Poincaré, for example, has not been overcome.

We may then take this attitude toward the first class of *a priori* objections to the mechanical ideal, namely: that if no definition of the terms in which we have presented this ideal is beyond danger of attack, yet no one inadequacy need be thought to remain beyond remedy.

Now let us turn to the second class of *a priori* objections. They are advanced by the heirs to the Aristotelian doctrine that "everything in nature takes place for the sake of an end." It is not easy to determine just how broad and just how narrow was the "nature" contemplated by Aristotle, nor yet to what extent things taking place for the sake of an end were also, in his view, parts of a mechanism. But in the sequel the possession of a nature that could be defined in the terms of the end sought and "always or for the most part" attained, was frequently enough supposed to demonstrate the inadequacy of mechanical explanation. Thus Aquinas: "We see that certain things lacking perception, *sci.* natural bodies, act for the sake of an end. . . But things which have no perception can only tend toward an end if directed by a conscious and intelligent being. Therefore there is an intelligence, by which all natural things are ordered to an end."[1]

The most significant modern representative of the point of view which Aristotle sought to make final is the science of biology. It was in this field, it will be remembered, that Kant imagined the demonstration of the inadequacy of mechanism to be complete. "It is quite certain," he writes, "that we can never adequately know, still less explain, organisms and their intrinsic possibility in terms of the purely mechanical principles of nature. This is so certain, indeed, that it is an absurdity for men even to make the attempt, or to hope that another Newton may arise who could make so much as the production of a blade of grass intelligible in terms of natural laws not directed by a purpose. An insight of this kind must be absolutely denied us."[2]

Perhaps the most helpful way of studying the present attitude of biology toward this question is to sketch its recent history, or at least a typical phase of that history. There is nothing more characteristic of the mechanical ideal in its practical working out than the effort to divide the larger bodies with which our experience presents us into

[1] *Summa theol.*, I, quæst. 2, art. 3.
[2] *Kr. d. Urtheilskraft*, p. 75.

spatial parts, to accord to these parts as few attributes as possible, then to seek to reconstruct the original body out of these *primordia rerum.* In biology the structure that first suggested itself as a convenient unit of composition was the cell, and the method which considered the cell to be related to the organism as the Democritian atom is related to the body composed of such atoms has been called the "cell theory." The distinct formulation of the cell theory goes back to Schleiden and Schwann. In 1838 Schleiden, confining his attention to plants, writes: "Each cell leads a double life, an independent one pertaining to its own development alone, and another incidental in so far as it has become an integral part of the plant." In 1839 Schwann extends the concept to all organisms: "Each cell is within certain limits an individual and independent whole. The vital phenomena of one are repeated entirely or in part in all the rest. These individuals, however, are not arranged side by side as an aggregate, but so operate together in a manner unknown to us as to produce an harmonious whole." And again, "The whole organism subsists only by means of the reciprocal action of the single elementary parts."[1]

Except for an occasional vagueness, such as the

[1] Taken from Whitman, "Inadequacy of the Cell Theory of Development," *Journal of Morphology,* Vol. viii, pp. 639 ff.

reference to "an harmonious whole," and except for the substitution of the "life" of a cell for the mere "existence" of an atom, the preceding description might have served Newton to depict the anatomy and physiology of all physical bodies, merely changing "cell" into "atom."

Of course, the cell theory is not yet mechanical, since it merely assumes the living cell, and in connection with it implies terms of description and explanation not immediately susceptible of mechanical definition, nor even of physico-chemical definition. Yet since the phenomena of cell life are to a much greater extent capable of a physico-chemical treatment than those of the organism as a whole, it is natural that the cell theory should be looked upon by those who defend it, as well as by those who oppose it, as an effort in the direction of mechanical explanation, and that it should seem to an onlooker that a biology which found itself to be drifting away from the cell theory had abandoned the hope of mechanical explanation in its field. That biology is taking this course is the view of some of its most prominent representatives.

The writers in question, differing as they do on points of detail, are at least agreed on this proposition: We know no laws of the individual cell or of the interaction of cells such as would explain the behavior of that composit of cells we call an organism. Some, at least, of the laws of the organism must treat it as indivisible. A favorite figure of those who take this standpoint,—the "organism standpoint," as Whitman calls it,—is borrowed from chemistry. "It can be shown, I think," says Morgan, "with some probability, that the forming organism is of such a kind that we can better understand its action when we consider it as a whole and not simply as the sum of a vast number of smaller elements. To draw . . . a rough parallel; just as the properties of sugar are peculiar to the molecule and can not be accounted for as the sum total of the properties of the atoms of carbon, hydrogen, and oxygen of which the molecule is made up, so the properties of the organism are connected with its whole organization and are not simply those of its individual cells, or lower units."[1] So Whitman compares the organism of many cells to a complex molecule: "The complex unit bears not only the structure of its individual parts, but also a totally new structure formed by the union of these parts."[2]

The concrete facts which these statements are intended to summarize are these:

1. The relation between two structures, which the biologist calls "homology," may exist between

[1] *Regeneration*, p. 278.
[2] Whitman, *loc. cit.*, p. 641.

a unicellular and a multicellular body. "So far as homology is concerned, the existence of cells may be ignored."[1]

2. In the process of development a unicellular organ may replace in one organism a multicellular organ in another. The laws of growth of an organism must be formulated in terms of the organism as a whole, and not in terms of its cells, if we are to have "continuity of organization." "Continuity of organization means only that definite structure foundation must be taken as the starting-point of each organism, and that the organism is not multiplied by cell division but rather continued as an individuality through all the stages of transformation and subdivision in the cells."[2]

3. The important phenomena of regeneration.

(*a*) The phenomena of "polarity": "We find that a piece of a bilateral animal regenerates a new anterior end from the part that lay nearer to the anterior end of the original animal, a new right side from the part that was nearest the original right side, and a new dorsal part from the region that lay near the original dorsal part, etc." Since the character of the cells constituting the two surfaces of a single section cannot greatly differ, the

[1] Whitman, *loc. cit.*, p. 645.
[2] *Ibid.*, p. 646.

nature of the growth on them must be due to the "structural relation of each to the whole to which each belongs." [1]

(b) The rate of growth: For example, in the growth of the tail of a fish after an oblique section, that part is found to grow the faster which has the greater growth to accomplish before it recovers its normal proportion to the other dimensions of the original. "These results show very clearly that in some way the development of the typical form of the tail influences the rate of growth at different points. Although the physiological conditions would seem to admit the maximum rate of growth over the entire cut-edge, this only takes place in those parts that give the new tail its characteristic form." [2]

So much for the organism standpoint and the concrete facts upon which it is based. Whether it does or does not present an obstacle to the realization of a mechanical ideal, depends upon the way in which it is interpreted, and, so far as I can discover, three constructions have been put upon it.

1. The cell being unsuitable to serve as a biological element which, itself without organization, produces an organism by division, combination, and

[1] Morgan, *op. cit.*, p. 280.
[2] *Ibid.*, p. 133.

interaction, a smaller unit is sought. "If the formative processes cannot be referred to cell division, to what can they be referred?. . . The answer to our question . . . will find the secret of organization, growth, and development not in cell formation, but in those ultimate elements of living matter for which *idiosomes* seems to me an appropriate name. What these idiosomes are . . . is the problem."[2] Such an outcome means that the organization standpoint is far from being a step away from the mechanical ideal; instead of posing the problem of physico-chemical explanation when analysis has been carried as far back as the cell, the whole discussion is postponed until we arrive at the "idiosome." So understood, the organization standpoint means to correct, not the ideal of a biological unit, but the identification of the cell with that unit.

2. A second point of view is that defined latterly by Driesch, to whom the phenomena we have referred to as "organic" appeal with particular force. The laws of regeneration and growth are not to be found in the properties of the cell, nor of any smaller organic element, nor of the inorganic constituents of organic matter. They "do not fall within any type of law known to the inorganic sciences, but require us to assume a new, peculiar,

[2] Whitman, *loc. sit.*, p. 657.

and peculiarly evidenced kind of elementary (that is, not further analyzable) law, and this necessity results from the fact that no physico-chemical mechanism can be imagined by means of which the phenomena in question can be reproduced."[1] The observations upon which Driesch bases so important a conclusion are not particularly recondite. Organisms can be found which have the following properties: (1) from any part the whole may be regenerated; (2) any part may be made to yield any part of the regenerated whole.[2] These characteristics give rise to two reflections. In the first place, the phenomenon of regeneration here studied can not be subsumed under physico-chemical laws. For, observe the regeneration of any segment: at some point of the segment differentiation begins. If we are to explain the process in physico-chemical terms, either this point must differ in physico-chemical structure from its neighbors, or it must be differently stimulated from without. But the latter alternative is easily excluded by experimental control. Nor can the former be true, since any neighboring point could have been made the seat of differentiation by properly choosing the site of section. In the second place, the laws which the pro-

[1] "Die Lokalisation morphogenetischer Vorgänge," *Archiv f. Entwickelungsmechanik der Oganismen*, Vol. viii, p. 99.

[2] To both of these statements there are obvious limits, which, however, do not affect the present discussion. Cf. *loc. cit.*, p. 72 f.

cess of regeneration actually does obey are not mechanical, as may be seen from the following analysis of them:

Suppose we were given the problem, to predict the point at which differentiation would occur in a given case. What data should we need, and what type of formula should we make use of? We should have to know (1) the type of organism to which the experimental fragment belonged, (2) the stage of the growth of each part operated upon, and (3) the site of the operation. We may, I take it, conceive the first data to be given as a system of ratios, each point in the organism being characterized by the ratios of its distance from certain determinate points (say the poles of the axis or axes of symmetry). Such ratios are obviously independent of the absolute size of the mature organism, or of any other peculiarity of the individual case experimented upon. The second data is given in the same way, though, unlike the first, it depends on time as a variable, or at least upon the typical ratio of the time taken to acquire a given form to the time taken to attain the typical form represented in (1). For any given experimental case, data (1) and (2) are evidently of the nature of fixed parameters, and the point of differentiation will depend on (3), the site of the operation, as the only variable. We may readily imagine the working out of the formula in an illustrative case. Suppose the segment resulting from the experimental operation were a tube, and that the first differentiation "necessary to pass from this form to the type-form (1)" were recognized to be a constriction of the tube: we may imagine that our formula would yield us a coefficient dependent upon (1) and (2) and an absolute dimension, say the length of the single axis of symmetry from section to section, determined by (3). We should then locate the constriction at a distance from one pole of the axis equal to a fractional part of the whole length of the axis, the value of this fraction being the coefficient calculated from the formula.

A science which makes use of such formulæ as the foregoing must be, in Driesch's opinion, *sui generis*.

There are many points in Driesch's article that would make interesting topics for discussion, *e. g.*, his conception of the "type" as the "end" of regeneration and growth, to attain which a given differentiation is "necessary"; but the whole concept of end and of necessary means is better left for another occasion when it may be given fuller treatment.[1] For the present, we may content ourselves with examining the two main theses of the argument

[1] *Vid.* p. 261 sqq., ''On Final Causes.''

as now explained. The first maintained that whatever the laws determining differentiation might be, they *could not be* physico-chemical; the second supposed itself in possession of these laws, and pointed out that they *were not* physico-chemical.

As to the first, let it be admitted that there is no difference definable in physico-chemical terms between the point at which differeniation takes places and its fellows. There is yet a difference definable in geometrical terms, and with this must come a difference in the kind of stimuli affecting the point.[1] A somewhat analogous case is presented in the phenomenon of magnetism. Any point of a soft iron core may be made a pole by properly sectioning the piece, yet the piece of iron is physico-chemically homogenous and we select a uniform magnetic field. It is exactly its geometrical peculiarity that differentiates the physical conditions at this point from those obtaining at neighboring points.

The second consideration points to the laws that determine differentiation, and shows them to be not physico-chemical in their nature. The chief distinction is that these laws state the processes taking place at one point to be a function of its geo-

[1] We here accept Driesch's contention that the stimulation of a point by its neighbors is as much to be accounted stimulus (as opposed to a structure) as is the stimulation from causes quite independent of the organism.

metrical relation to other remote points, making no mention of the structures separating these points.[1]

Here, in insisting on the fact that the laws of biology do neglect certain details, I think Driesch has put his finger on that which characterizes biology as a science, and the peculiar way in which this elimination is effected ought to serve as a definition of this science.[2] But the fact that by a process of elimination we can obtain laws in which new kinds of data are demanded, new kinds of formulæ used, does not mean that we have a new science, or, in the terminology of this article, does not show that we have introduced a new dimension. Nothing is more common in the handling of purely mechanical problems than to effect just this kind of elimination. Thus, to take one case, by calling approximately rigid connections absolutely rigid, we are able in mechanical systems to "eliminate" coördinates, that is, to neglect detail. As a result of such elimination, we frequently obtain formulæ which introduce new terms. The law, "the work we can get out of a machine is equal to the work we put into it," is such a formula, and can be applied in

[1] This I take to be the chief outcome of Driesch's demonstration of vitalism. His use of the concept ''action at a distance'' is a help to the imagination to which the author is entitled if he be not confused thereby, and I see no evidence that Driesch has attached any undue importance to the device.

[2] *Cf.* pp. 261 sqq., 56, 60-64, 109-111.

practice to the measure of internal work without considering at all the construction of the machine.

In a word, Driesch does not show psysico-chemical explanation to break down in the field of biology, and does not convince us that the formulæ here used are other than such as would result from eliminating detail in the physico-chemical process, after a fashion perfectly familiar to us.

3. The foregoing criticism of Driesch may be taken as a fitting introduction to the third interpretation of the organism view,—the one which, so far as the present writer has observed, is the most common among the biologists of the day. This view admits the existence of laws peculiar to biology, making it for the present an independent science in the sense that no knowledge of the physics and chemistry of the cell or of any other unit will enable us to replace these laws in the business of prediction. But though these laws may at present be indispensable and irreducible, though they may be permanently true and useful, the establishment of their existence can not constitute a "demonstration" of the vitalistic standpoint in the sense urged by Driesch. In spite of the absence of a physico-chemical explanation of such phenomena, is there any reason to suppose such an explanation to be impossible? Morgan sums up the data upon which

we can base an answer, as follows. (1) The action of poisons, the formation of galls, the effect of lithium salts (Herbst), changes due to light, gravity, contact, etc., are best understood from the physico-chemical standpoint. (2) The effect of "internal" factors is less easily brought under this point of view. Thus the growth of an egg "we find difficult, if not impossible, to attribute to external causes, yet . . . the first steps through which this takes place can be referred to physico-causal principles. These are the separation of the piece from the whole; the change of the unsymmetrical piece into a symmetrical one, brought about, in part at least, by contractile phenomena in the piece, aided, no doubt, in some cases by surface tension, etc. . . . We find here the beginning of physico-causal change, and . . . we have no reason to suppose that at one step in the process this passes into the vitalistic causal principle." Having insisted upon the present impossibility of offering a complete physico-chemical explanation, the author concludes: "We shall, therefore, call ourselves vitalists? . . . I see no ground for accepting a vitalistic principle that is not a physico-causal one, but perhaps a different one from any known at present to the physicist or chemist."[1]

[1] *Op. cit.*, p. 285 ff.

The preceding sketch of a certain phase of development in biological science has been given in the belief that here, if anywhere in experience, we must look for whatever facts may promise ultimately to resist mechanical explanation. If such facts were unanimously urged by the leading biologists of the day, one would still accept their conclusion with caution, realizing how difficult it would be to form an opinion as to what is "ultimately" possible and impossible. But as it is, the weight of technical opinion,—and of that branch of technical opinion most impressed with the error of certain hasty steps leading too directly toward the *quasi*-mechanical theory of life processes,—the weight of this opinion will recognize neither a "demonstration" nor a balance of probability in favor of the failure of the mechanical ideal. If a layman may venture to estimate the best biological opinion, it would sum up to this: Laws which are not mechanical, such as those having reference to ends (Pflüger and Wolff), and those employing concepts like *actio in distans* (Driesch), are valuable in biology and make prediction possible where it would not be possible if we were to confine ourselves to mechanical terms; but this value is either temporary, while we await a better mechanical insight (Haacke), or if permanent, it is in the nature of an economic device. In any case, the existence of non-mechanical laws does not excuse us from the search for more fundamental mechanical laws; still less does it give us assurance that such a search must remain permanently unsuccessful.

The writer has advanced the opinion that if the inadequacy of the mechanical ideal cannot be demonstrated from those aspects of nature studied by the biologist, then in no other region of experience can we expect to find such a demonstration. This opinion must be left for the present as a conjecture based on experience; the present paper does not pretend to have exhausted all the historical motives that have led thinkers to oppose the mechanical ideal. For example, it takes no account of the large body of opinion which opposes to the mechanical, not another kind of law (teleological, vitalistic), but the alternative of no law at all. In some aspects the doctrine of *liber arbitrium* would have to be so interpreted.[1] But these more general problems would carry us beyond the regions we could profitably discuss in brief space. We must, then, be content with the best examples of opposition to a mechanical ideal with which history presents us, and pass on to a new question. If, namely, we can find in experience no obstacle

[1] Perhaps the standpoint taken by Renouvier and Prat in their *Nouvelle monadologie* may be taken as giving the most systematic presentation. On this see the author, PHILOSOPHICAL REVIEW, Vol. viii, p. 638 f.

to our progress in the direction indicated by the mechanical ideal, can we find any reason for supposing this progress to be necessarily continuous? Or, again, if we were to attain the goal defined, should we have reached the final solution of the problem of explanation? In a word, if there is no justification in present knowledge for predicting the failure of the mechanical ideal, is there any safer ground for predicting its success? But this chapter of the discussion must, as has been said, be reserved for a future occasion.

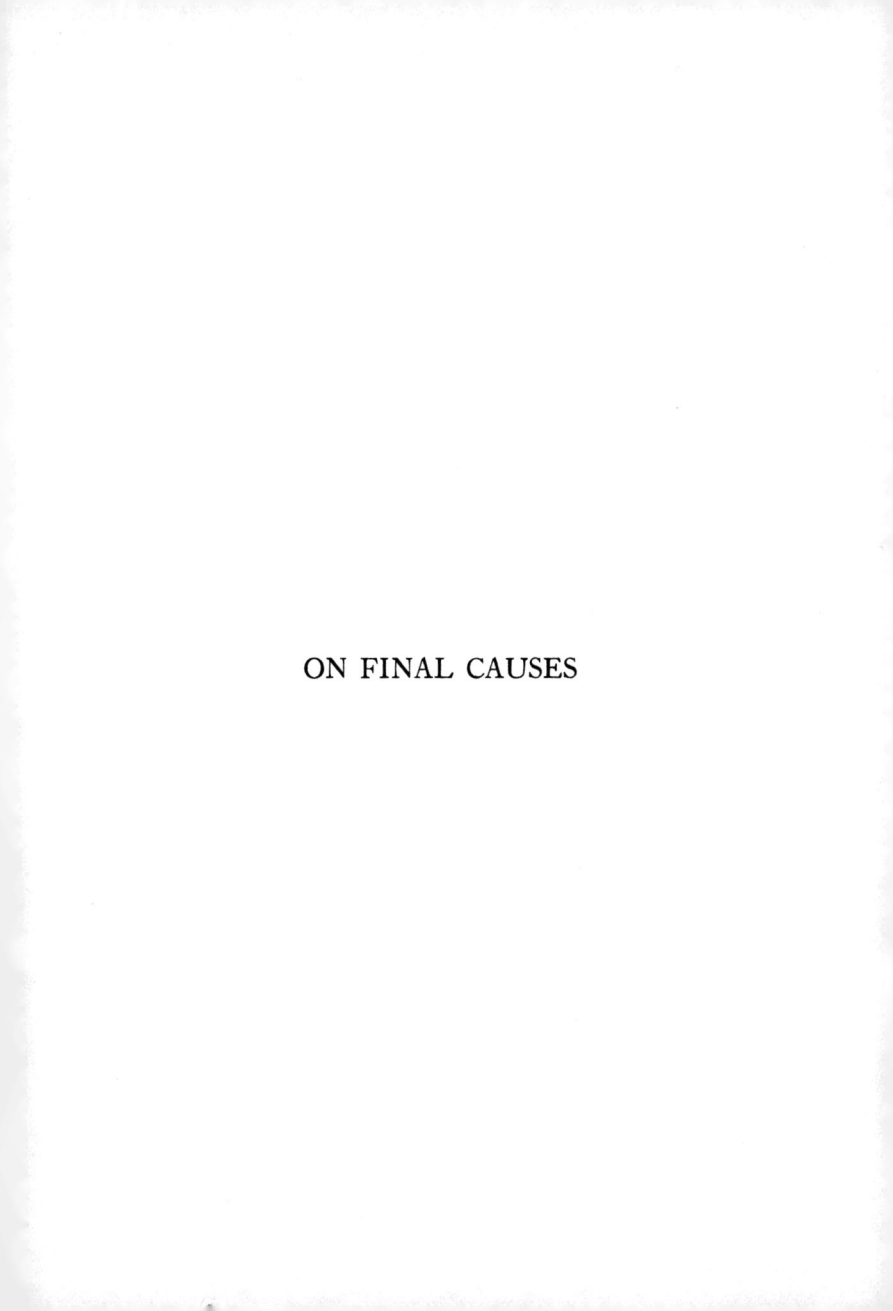

ON FINAL CAUSES

XII.

ON FINAL CAUSES

An Abstract

If nature were reducible to a mechanical system, would "ends" be definable in terms of such a system? Could they be treated as "causes"? Could "teleological explanation" retain any claim to a place among the objective methods of science?

An objective method of explanation is not necessarily one that is indispensable to prediction. A method plainly dependent upon a selective grouping of the phenomena to be explained may still be objective, if it can be shown to ensure an economy in the describing and explaining of these phenomena. Its objectivity depends upon the universality of the motive of selection, and not on the absence of selection.

Simple examples can be drawn from the "special" physical sciences in which the economy of a selective method of description and explanation may be demonstrated in terms of the mechanical system within which selection is made. *E. g.*, thermo-dynamics is a "special" science because the statement of its laws involves the non-mechanical dimension "temperature." The mechanical reconstruction of the phenomena of heat reduces temperature to a function of the velocity of concealed mass-motions. Yet this reduction made, the laws of thermo-dynamics still remain true and its special method objective, for the reason that the science deals with the mechanical elements of the system in large groups. Temperature, namely, is a function of *average* velocities, and by the methods of averages we are able to omit mechanical detail while losing nothing of scientific rigor.

Turning now to the teleological method, it may be shown that in the judgment, A is B in order that C may be D, the "end" CD cannot serve as the necessary and sufficient condition of the means AB: the distinction between teleology and mechanism *would be lost*. And lost it has been in the history of science. The "integral" (Hamiltonian) form of the fundamental formula of mechanics has been taken for a teleological type in which the "end" constituted the necessary and sufficient condition of the means; but it differs from the "differential" (Legrangian) form only in mathematical expression. Teleology, to remain distinct from mechanism, must leave something out. This is does by establishing an average relation between cause and effect. The "end" thus appears as a consequence which *on the average* follows on the means. And this is the historical (*e. g.*, Aristotelian) habit of thought on the subject.

To define the "end," it is necessary selectively to group mechanical phenomena. The "end" is then to be determined as follows: (1) It is the average effect of a class of causes, differing from the mechanical effect (*a*) in that it is essentially an average and not a universal effect, and (*b*) in that there need be no mechanical likeness between the causes producing the same effect. (2) In any given case, the cause in accomplishing an end produces also an infinite number of other results throughout the universe. The "end" is distinguished from these secondary results, in that causes which accomplish like ends do not produce secondary results having any resemblance *inter se*, except, of course, in that they all illustrate in their atomic behavior the mechanical law of the system.

From this definition of an end, the sense in which it may determine means, and so be treated as cause, may be readily deduced. The economy of the method depends on the success with which it omits mechanical detail and yet serves as a means of prediction. With this economy is established the objective validity of teleology.

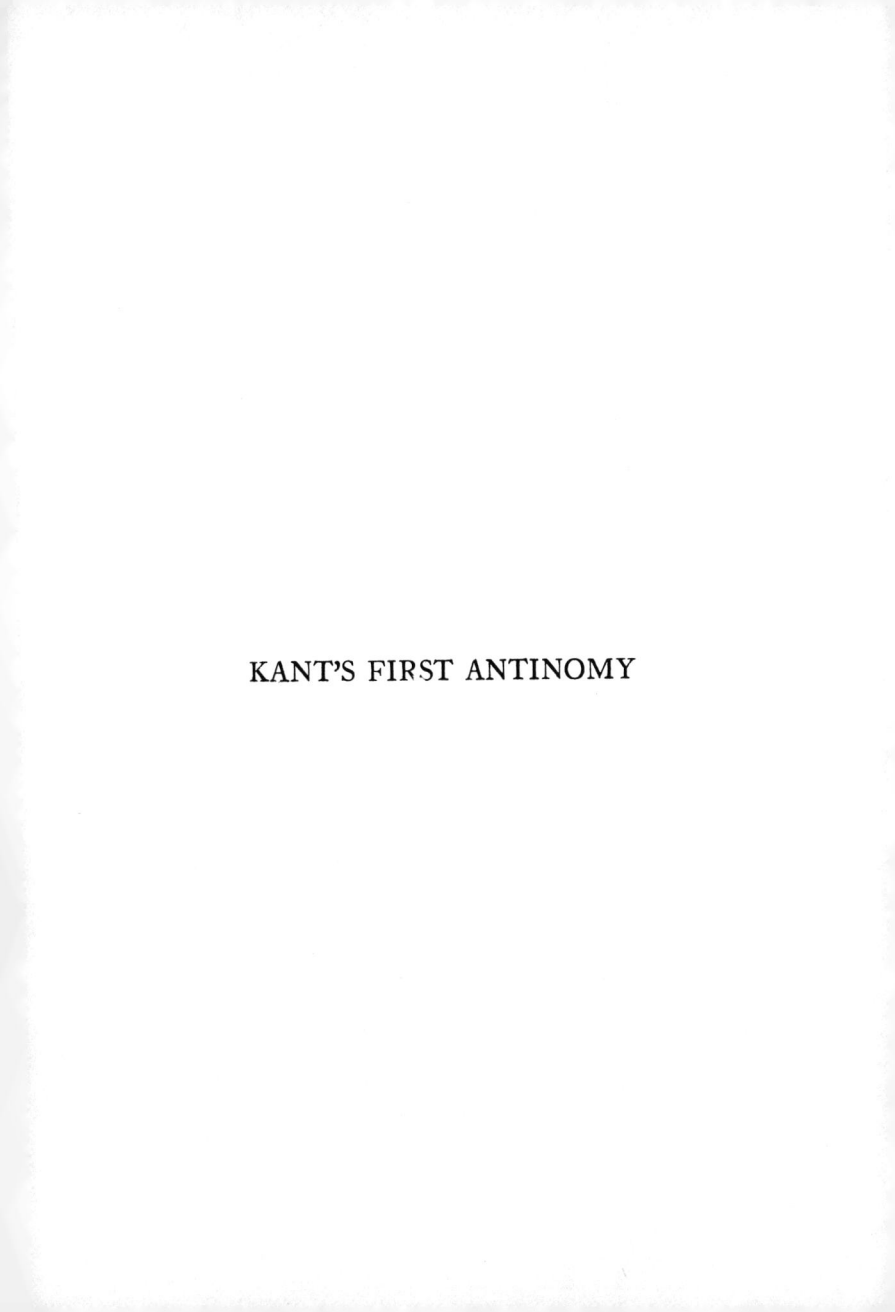

KANT'S FIRST ANTINOMY

XIII.

KANT'S FIRST ANTINOMY[1]

The Question of Fact

PERHAPS no one would take quite seriously, argument by argument, Kant's presentation of the "first antinomy." It may not, that is, have been made out impossible to think of a world infinite in extent, equally impossible to think of one that is finite; forbidden to conceive of a world whose past history has no beginning, no less forbidden to conceive of one whose past history has a first moment.

Yet out of the "much argument" there may be seen to emerge a puzzle not without its own suggestion. It is this: There is no method by which we may determine the spread of bodies in space, the history of their behavior in time, save that of bare observation. There are, however, the most plausible reasons for asserting that the observations indispensable to this determining form an endless series. If now there is but one method of settling an issue of fact, and if *that* method will not settle it, are we not face to face with the most puzzling of conceptions, *an unknowable fact?*

[1] Read before the Baltimore meeting of the American Philosophical Association, December, 1908.

One naturally thinks first of establishing the reality of the issue. *Is* an infinite series of experiments, one asks, indispensable to the answering of these two questions of extent and duration? Here, many reflections occur to a modern that have received no consideration at the hands of Kant.

The two questions present unequal difficulties. Those connected with the problem of the space-distribution of bodies are certainly the less vital, yet they should be set forth in some manner. Thus, it may occur to one that Kant has made an assumption requiring analysis when he thinks of the method by which we determine the existence of bodies at a certain distance from the earth (say) as involving a consumption of time proportionate to the distance. Certainly if the only method were to send a messenger to such regions, or to await a messenger (say, of light) from them, then, however rapidly the messenger might travel, a measurable time would be required for him to arrive and report. And as the journey must be infinite in order to exhaust the infinite reaches of space, the time involved would be infinite no less.

If that were all! But the consideration thrusts itself upon us at this point that not all physical influences are known to be propagated. The gravitational effect of one mass upon another is, so far as experiment can decide, instantaneous. If so, it is conceivable that the presence of masses at all distances from a given finite system should be reflected in the momentary behavior of this system. In order that such a state of affairs may result, however, the law of the force which one body exerts on another must be such that no two distributions could give the same map of lines of force in a given finite region. But so far as gravitation is concerned, there are at least certain "critical cases" in which more than one, in fact an infinite number of distributions of mass would give exactly the same force-map for a circumscribed region. One such case would be that in which the region in question lay inside of a spherical shell. The intensity in the interior of such a shell being zero, it follows that the presence of the shell would not be revealed by any momentary behavior of systems lying within it. To assure ourselves of its presence or absence, we should require some other method than that of obseerving the gravitational behavior of a finite system of bodies.[1]

[1] To be sure, the theorem establishing the zero intensity of gravitational force in the interior of a spherical shell depends upon the assumption of the law of the inverse square. To establish the theorem that *no* law of nature can be defined which reflects distribution throughout an infinite region in the behavior of bodies in a finite region requires two steps. First, a law must be conceived that yields no such critical cases as that defined by the law of gravitation. Second, such a law must give a force-function that lies at a finite distance from any given force-function which yields such critical cases. Otherwise, viewed

If then no law of the interaction of bodies is empirically known which would enable us in a finite number of experiements to determine the distribution of bodies throughout space by examining the behavior of bodies within a finite region, we can have no quarrel with Kant's results. Whether bodies are distributed throughout the infinity of space or are confined to a region of it remains an experimentally unanswerable question.

But when we turn from the problem of distribution in space to that of history in time, the facile analogy by which Kant himself is wont to pass from the one question to the other seems something too unconsidered. For we have undoubtedly the vague suspicion that the history of the past is embodied in the *now* in a much more complete way than the structure of the *yonder* is reflected in the *here*.

I am not inclined to stick on the point that the history of the past is a present document,—is, as Hume would say, a lively idea associated with a present impression. I am rather tempted to put the question, Whether or not the history, however

the necessity of a probable error of observation, an infinite number of observations would be required to decide between the function that does and the function that does *not* reflect an infinite distribution in a finite one. I am content to leave so delicate a question of mathematics to future treatments of the problem. The difficulties of the discussion seem to me out of proportion to the importance of the issue.

recorded, of a system is indispensable to a prediction of its future conduct.

When Kant suggests that past history throws its light upon present conditions (a light indispensable to our vision into the future) he is proposing no new idea, nor one likely to offend the commonest of common-sense. Only, the sciences in which retrospect is necessary to prevision are the relatively superficial sciences,—biology, sociology, psychology. The adjective "superficial" is not of course meant to be abusive. It is obvious that certain sciences owe their claim upon our attention to their success in inventing types of explanation readily applicable when the data for applying more thorough-going sciences is wanting. For example, few would be prepared to maintain that the training of an organism left no trace on the intimate anatomy of that organism, although it is true no such trace has been observed. We have not advanced beyond the stage in which the anatomical changes effected by training are referred to in figures borrowed from other sciences; we still confine ourselves to speaking of the "well-worn paths" of association and the like. Such expressions only give name to a hope and a faith, but they do at least testify to that much,—to a faith, namely, that did we know enough of minute structural differences we should be able to predict a difference in the reactions of two organisms to the same stimulus when these organisms, as we now view them, are unlike only in training. Not knowing so much in the way of structural detail, we must include among the data indispensable to prediction a knowledge of the past history of the organism, and we introduce among the influences of which account must be taken in explaining behavior "the force of habit," "the burden of memory," and like expressions which in their very wording mimic the categories of mechanical explanation. To have invented such devices for a ready prediction where the data required by more general and underlying sciences is lacking is just the contribution of those sciences I have called "superficial." But we must recognize that such sciences are conscious of their superficial, make-shift character; that they have themselves the ambition to dispense with their special devices, and their first step in this sense would be to eliminate if possible an appeal to past history as necessary to prediction.

We cannot say, of course, that any given scientific ideal is bound to be realized by a complaisant world of fact. It is perhaps true that biology has made some progress in its effort to trace the structural modifications wrought in an organism by its experience. On the other hand, an increasing knowledge of the inanimate world has revealed, where we least expected to find them, classes of phenomena in which

KANT'S FIRST ANTINOMY: THE QUESTION OF FACT

account has to be taken of past history. One which has suggested more frequently than any other that puzzling phrase "the memory of matter," is the well-known phenomenon of "hysteresis." It would appear, *e. g.*, that two magnets in exactly the same present condition would react differently to the same treatment if they had come into that condition by different ways. In other words, we have to know the past history of a magnet, just as we do of an organism, if we are able to predict its future behavior. Of course if instances of this kind should multiply in the inorganic world, and if in the organic world science should ultimately give up its hope of dispensing with the kind of explanation we have called "superficial," the *now* would no more embody the *then* than th*e here* reflects the *yonder*, and Kant's transition from the problem of space distribution to that of past history would be beyond criticism. But as just the opposite is the case, it is no idle indulgence, but a pressing requirement of sound method to reconsider Kant's treatment of history.

How different from the problem of recovering a *living* past may be that of establishing a world's age! Different indeed it must be from the point of view of an image of nature which regards its history as completely recounted if we substitute negative values of time in a formula *now* observed to

KANT'S FIRST ANTINOMY: THE QUESTION OF FACT

hold throughout the known world, and solve for all the dependent variables. And as of the past, so of the future,—but for a change of sign.

While such an assumption vastly simplifies our conception of natural science, it complicates or rather subtilizes beyond expectation the particular problem with which we are here dealing. Questions not easy to answer begin to crowd upon us. What sort of a formula would mean an infinite past history? What sort a finite? What kind of experiment would be necessary and sufficient to decide between the two formulas? Would this experiment involve a finite or an infinite series of observations?

The first question is not difficult to answer, so little difficult indeed that a formula which means an *infinite* past and an *infinite* future history is the one which every scientist carries around with him as the more or less conscious starting-point of his reflections on natural philosophy. Arrhenius, for example, does not hesitate to say that no other world-view is to him conceivable than such as makes past history infinite. All such formulas have at least this in common: they succeed in expressing everything that varies in nature (positions in space, velocities, electric charges, magnetic poles) as functions of a single variable, called time, so that for all real values of this independent variable we obtain real values for at least one kind of the dependent variables (*e. g.*, position) and values greater than zero for the time-rate of change of at least one kind of these variables (*e. g.*, velocity). A system of gravitating masses with certain velocities normal to the lines connecting the masses would be a system with an infinite past, and we might superimpose upon such a system various phenomena of radiation which would not preclude such infinity.

Neither would the attempt to construct an image of a system with a *finite* past or future history seem to offer insuperable difficulty. Perhaps it will lie nearer to our experience to think first of a system destined to run down in a finite time. To this end nothing more seems required than to adapt the *Wärmetod*, which Clausius conceived to be the future actually awaiting the system we know. Suppose in a gravitating system we imagine the masses to behave as though moving through a resisting medium. One effect would be constantly to diminish the velocities normal to the radii vectores of the system, velocities now conceived to remain constant. The consequence would be a gradual approach along a spiral path of satellites toward planets, of planets toward suns, of suns toward each other. If the following of such paths resulted in impact with velocities greater than zero, even if we assumed the masses to be perfectly elastic, the conditions would require that the kinetic energy of the masses of the system should gradually diminish, while such gain in potential energy as could be established would not be sufficient to make up the loss; so that the whole system would tend toward a zero of energy, *i. e.*, toward a state of inactivity. To be sure, so far as experience acquaints us with systems of masses moving through resisting mediums, we look to phenomena of the medium, such as convection currents and radiation effects, to keep the total of energy constant. But nothing assures us so long as there is an error of observation that the sum will be made up, and if it be not, one form of change does not completely replace another; the whole history of the system, which is precisely a record of its changes, tends toward an end.

There remains a point to be considered, or rather two points. A system tending toward equilibrium may not so approach the limit as to attain to it in a finite time. And, in the second place, since we are inspired to these reflections by Kant's treatment of the antinomies, we are without interest in images constructed in terms of laws of force which a finite number of experiments could prove to be untrue to fact. But I am content to treat these two problems in geometrical form. If we construct a graph of the energy of a system in which this quantity remained constant, laying off time along the x-axis, and the corresponding energy along the Y, the energy would be represented by a line parallel to the x-axis. The fact that there is always an experimental error makes it, however, impossible to distinguish between this parallel and a second straight line which would intersect the x axis at a point representing the time when the energy of the system had become zero. As this state of affairs remains unchanged so long as the probable error is greater than zero, and as the very formula by means of which we express the probable error of experimental results implies that nothing short of an infinite series of experiments would enable us to reduce such an error to zero, it follows that no finite series would enable us to exclude the possibility of a *finite* future history. On the other hand it might be that without going outside of the types of curve which we are accustomed to regard as alone capable of expressing physical laws, we could find none lying within the limits of probable error which did not intersect the axis of x. We should still not have excluded the possibility of an *infinite* future. For unless the forces we can ascribe to the system are very different from any with which we are acquainted, the energy of the system must increase with the separation of its parts in space. But we have already accepted Kant's result that no finite series of experiments could determine this distribution for us. Consequently, though we were able to establish a law which would require any *finite* system to run down in a finite time, we could not establish the finitude of the system we call the world.

The problem of a finite future has been presented first, in deference to our prejudices. Conceptually, however, there is no greater difficulty in defining the conditions of a finite past. The transition from the one to the other involves nothing more complicated than a change of sign, the substitution of an accelerating medium for a retarding. It is true that experience makes the latter concept less familiar to us, but it can render it no more difficult to define. To go forward to an end and to go backward to a beginning are problems of the same order.

I have expressed, then, as well as the extreme difficulties of the problem would permit, the opinion that Kant is essentially right, that no possible experiment could decide the issue between a finite distribution of bodies in space and an infinite; between a finite world-history and an infinite. The question remains: What of it?

It need hardly be said that no one who deals with such a question is tempted to his task by interest in a world's destiny. The game is finite enough so far as he is concerned, and his curiosity respecting the fate of the theatre of his brief act must be trifling.

KANT'S FIRST ANTINOMY: THE QUESTION OF FACT

The real question that does excite the interest of reflection is that on which Kant focuses our attention: Is not the issue between these two alternatitve assumptions purely one of fact, and is not the fact involved unknowable? Must there not then be such a thing as an unascertainable fact, one lying beyond the reach of all possible experience, in a word a *Ding-an-sich?*

It will be remembered that Kant's own answer to the question: What then? was eminently practical. He saw in the situation nothing but the occasion to point a moral; one which took at his hands the form of a command: In your judgment of what the world is, take into account as much of its distribution in space, as much of its history in time as you can. Our considerations would only modify, and that but slightly, the form of the injunction. The omission from our calculation of a spatial presence leads to a *constant* error. The issue between a finite and an infinite history reduces so far as we can see to a question of the *probable* error of experiment. Our imperative would then become: Neglect no source of constant error, reduce the probable error of experiment more and more. All of which the laboratorius would be in haste to acclaim,—as a commonplace.

The interest of the problem seems to me to center in the light its discussion throws upon the question:

KANT'S FIRST ANTINOMY: THE QUESTION OF FACT

What is a fact? The answer Kant returns to this question makes him in his own eyes an idealist; but when that answer is stated in its clearest form, when the idealism implied by it is reduced to its simplest terms, one has the conviction that the Kant of the Dialectic is an idealist of a very different stripe from the Kant of the Æsthetic and the Analytic; that furthermore it is this Kant if any, who can define the meaning of a *Ding-an-sich*, and defend the right of such a concept to a place in an empirical idealism.

And Kant's solution of this particular puzzle respecting an unknowable fact would seem to reduce to this: It is the very nature of a fact to be unknowable; but unknowable only in the sense that an *ideal* is unattainable. That which as a "*Gegebenes*" refusing to be found would be a real puzzle from which the various mysticisms of a "*docta ignorantia*" might spring, when viewed as an "*Aufgegebenes*" becomes an ideal of method. Its appearance in the discussion has the value of stating briefly the distinction between a less true and a more true experimental result, and of pointing the corollary, that for every result taken for "true," there is always definable and always ascertainable a "truer."

If I am right in reinterpreting the "regulative principle" in which Kant's discussion culminates to mean, "reduce your probable error, eliminate more and more of the inexhaustible sources of constant error," the ideal fact is the empirical result whose probable error is zero and for which a source of constant error is not definable. The interest of the antinomy we have discussed consists not in the discovery of *one* question of fact whose decision lies beyond the reach of possible experience, but in the demonstration which it offers that *all* statements of fact must retain an expression for probable error and must yield a definition of possible sources of constant error. The "real" fact is an "ideal" which we can define only in terms of a method that possesses a device for distinguishing between the more and the less real.

In Kant's many treatments of the *noumenon*, there seems to me no statement of the necessity for retaining this concept so clear and so convincing as a passage of the section "Von dem Grunde der Unterscheidung, etc.": "Wo nicht ein beständiger Zirkel heraus kommen soll, das Wort Erscheinung schon eine Beziehung auf etwas anzeigt, dessen unmittelbare Vorstellung zwar sinnlich ist, was aber an sich selbst. . . . etwas, d. i. ein von der Sinnlichkeit unabhängiger Gegenstand sein muss." If there is, as Jacobi suggests, a difficulty in becoming a Kantian without retaining enough of a noumenon to make our word phenomenon mean something, it is a difficulty analogous to that which would arise in maintaining that all hands are right hands. If there is a difficulty in remaining Kantian because of this noumenon, it is owing to the mistaken inference that because a noumenon must be something different from *any* phemonenon, it must be defined without reference to a series of phenomena. Suppose one were to maintain that the method of distinguishing between the "appearance" and "that which appears" was one that defined and made attainable a "real" for every "appearing," only that this "real" was no less an "appearing" pointing to a "more real" and so on *in infinitum*. Here is no longer a circle but a progress, and if one defines the goal of this progress as an "ideal," it is none the less true that only a progress can define a *real ideal*. And it is only in the possibility of progress that one can be interested.

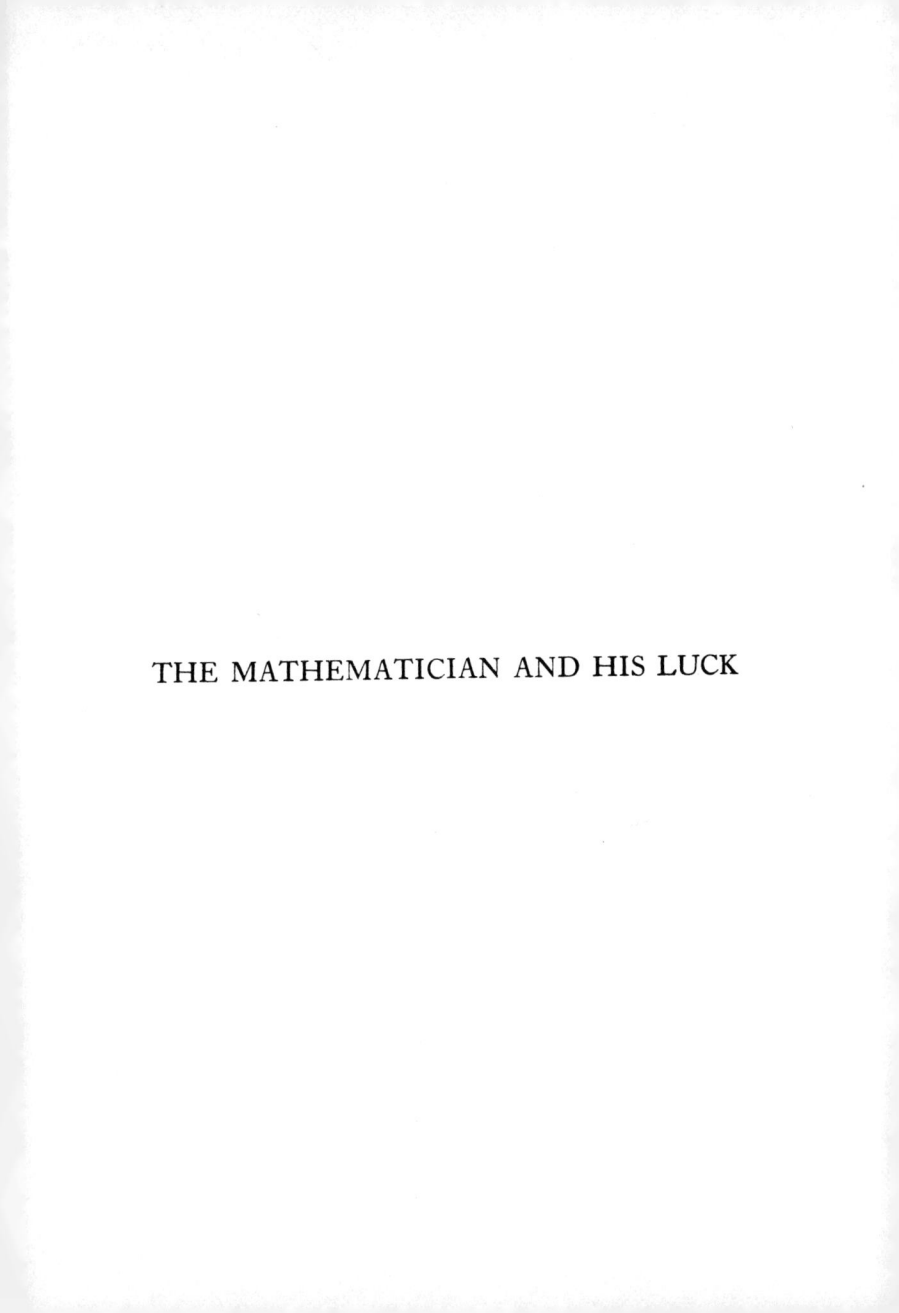

THE MATHEMATICIAN AND HIS LUCK

XIV.

THE MATHEMATICIAN AND HIS LUCK[1]

THE mathematician of the seventeenth century is a splendid figure of pride and self-satisfaction, for he believed himself to be the sole possessor of absolute truth. The mathematician of the twentieth century is a much less splendid but much more interesting fellow. Assurance has been replaced by skepticism, and satisfaction by discontent. Indeed the modern mathematician is the least happy and least contented of men,—out of sympathy with the universe, and out of humor with his luck. And that not because the gods who put the world together have treated him worse than his fellows. Just the opposite is the case. Of all possible worlds, have they not offered him just that one which is mathematically simplest, which can be described in terms of the easiest arithmetic, the easiest geometry, the easiest kinematics, and the slightest mechanics? The gods have been wonderfully good to the mathematician, and you would think that in this vale of

[1] Being an address read after a dinner of the Philadelphia Section of the Association of Teachers of Mathematics of the Middle States and Maryland.

tears he at least would be able to laugh. He is in luck, and it would seem as though he alone were in luck; for in a world as indifferent, ironical, tragic as is this one, the rest of us are not accustomed to find our ease considered, our desires filled. Indeed the deepest irony of all lies in the mathematical grace and eleganace of the machine the gods have devised for our undoing.

But is the mathematician grateful? Not he! The only lucky man in the world is unhappy just because he is in luck. He does not want his luck. He does not in his heart believe in it. He even goes so far as to suspect that there must be something wrong with himself or with his science or with his way of applying this science, that his position should be so happily anomalous. He would I think welcome any suggestion that would better his condition by making it worse and more human.

So at least I have made the mathematician out, and having made him out so, I thought there could be no more delicate and tactful way of thanking him for his hospitality on this occasion than by doing what I might to relieve him of this luck.

The dying eighteenth century brought forth in heavy travail many new and troubling things, but none newer and more upsetting than that philosophy of Kant which Moses Mendelssohn called "the all-disturbing." "A Copernican change of standpoint," was one of the expressions Kant himself found for the revolution which had taken place within him; and how apt the phrase, may be judged from a single passage of the *Kritik der reinen Vernunft* into which Kant has put all his meaning and all his daring,—"The order and uniformity of the phemonena we call nature we ourselves put there and never had we found them there had we not first put them there." The immediate followers of Kant developed this thought of the master by working out more completely the theory of *how* we put law into nature. They saw as Kant had not always seen that the imposing of such laws must be an act of the will, the expression of our choice and freedom. So, that experience which had been looked upon by the English school as a mere passive reception of facts, came to be regarded as a process of construction, a work of the creative imagination. "Every fact comes of an act," was Fichte's way of putting the result, and with this result whether right or wrong all later philosophy has had to reckon. Its bearing on our particular problem is obvious enough. There is no other way of freeing the mathematician from the curse of his luck than that of assuring him he made it himself. It is this idea I venture to put before you.

The point of departure for the idealistic philosophy of nature was the insight that nature and science are no more capable of independent definition than are right and left, above and below, husband and wife. Nature was still the object of scientific knowledge, but only in the sense that a goal or ideal may be the object of endeavor. Salomon Maimon suggested the figure, *limit of a series*. As the square root of two is defined by the terms of the series that approaches it, so is nature defined by the series of ever-broadening but always finite insights which make up science in its development. Nature, we may say, is that image which science approaches as the error of observation approaches zero. So viewed, nature is no *Ding-an-sich*, but the name of a certain ideal. Nature is completed science. Science is nature in the making.

If this analysis of meanings is accepted, one outcome is obvious,—the maker of science must be the maker of nature: and if the making of science is no mere passive receiving of hard facts, if on the contrary, this making is an act, an act of the creative imagination, then surely it should not surprise us that at least some aspects of the thing made should be after our heart's desire. This all follows *if* the scientist is permitted to use his imagination, *if* he is allowed to exercise choice. But is he? I can't help thinking that those who maintain the contrary have not lived in laboratories or observatories. They have imagined in the simplicity of their hearts that the experimenter could leave all to his experiment and do nothing himself. It would be beautiful if it were so, but no one knows better than the experimenter that his task is far from being as simple as all this comes to. He finds himself forced to choose between equally permissible images of what is going on around him. Every *laboratorius* knows this, but not every one realizes the range of choice left open to him. He accepts many choices that have already been made as though the issue were dead. It is to the revival of these issues that a historian of the exact sciences, a Mach let us say, contributes. Moreover the statement of all the alternative images between which choice must be made, is possible only in so far as these images have actually been constructed. It is to this construction that a mathematician of the order of a Poincaré contributes.

For these reasons the philosopher attaches great importance to studies which the experimental scientist is likely to view with impatience, namely the history or perhaps I should say the psychology of the sciences called "exact" and the activities of the mathematician constructing symbolisms of no immediate application. For these studies contribute more than any other to the emancipation of the scientist by actually making it possible to shatter the scheme of things and to remold it. They open the way to re-creations of nature.

Of the choices which reflection on the history and psychology of science has brought clearly to the consciousness of the scientist, there are two which are particularly important. The first is the choice between images in such wise analytically connected that we may pass from one to the other by a recognized transformation. Such is the relation between the Ptolemaic and the Copernican pictures of the solar system. The achievement of Copernicus involved no new observation. It was truly the work of a creative imagination.

But how elementary is the transformation of coördinates within the Euclidean system when compared with the transformation of the system itself into one of the non-Euclidean orders. Yet the advantages and disadvantages of such transformation have to be exhaustively considered before we can close the issue between them. Very recently too we have come to consider transformations that involve the relative motion of various systems of coördinates. One may consider what simplicity has been introduced into our description of the phenomena of nature by formulating the principle of relativity. May we not judge that we are only beginning to realize the scope and freedom of choices of this order, only beginning to understand our own omnipotence?

In the choices so far considered the alternate images are analytically connected. But there is another order of choice always forced upon the scientist that is something more than a transformation. It is the choice between the infinity of laws falling within the probable error of his scientific data. If Copernicus illustrates the importance of transformation, Newton gives an example of a choice within limits; for surely the essential part of Newton's contribution was his ability to formulate a single law not identical with but close enough to the separate inductions of Galileo and Kepler. The contribution of Newton as well as that of Copernicus was an act of imagination. Of course choice between limits raises an experimental issue. Between Newton on the one hand and Kepler and Galileo on the other, the choice is no longer open. But evidently as long as experimental error attaches to our data, the disappearance of an old issue is accompanied by the apearance of a new. It is for this reason that we can always treat the apparently complex as the really simple, by the assumption of concealed motions. Nor can this possibility ever be eliminated. Though the range within which our choice may be exercised were reduced to the size of a pin-point, this would still be a whole universe of freedom, freedom to suppose what relations we chose between the mathematical points within the pin-point. To this is due the development of those images of the concealed which we so crudely and inadequately lump together under the caption of atomic theories.

I have tried in this brief and sketchy way to suggest the sense in which the history of science is a history not merely of passive observation but also of creative imagination. We can see in what sense it is true "the heavens declare the glory of Kepler and Newton." And can we not see as well why the mathematician is so perfectly accommodated in a world he himself has made? I should like, if time permitted, to go further—O, much further. I should like to raise another question, one that I dare say every one of you is asking himself at this moment,—Why, if the mathematician has made his luck, has he not made more of it? Why isn't all science as simple as geometry? Perhaps I should answer by another question,—Why since Wordsworth made such beautiful poems did he not make more of them and make them more beautiful? Perhaps because it isn't easy to create; perhaps because it is even harder to make a world than it is Columbus-like to find one.

But I should like to have made this vague answer more definite. I should like to have suggested that our nature-building proceeds in a certain order. It is not unlike the old "fifteen-puzzle," which most of you will remember. Nothing was easier than to get the first few numerals in order. Then the thing grew harder and harder, until at the very end you generally decided it would be better to start all over again. I mean to suggest that in the making of science all that is resistant, complex, unlovely, is left to the late-comer; and that perhaps the way of correcting this will involve beginning all over again. In which case it may well enough turn out that the geometer's ease is just the disease from which the superimposed sciences suffer, that the mathematician's luck is by way of being a human misfortune, or rather an all-too-human mistake. But to follow these hints would be to turn after-dinner into before-breakfast. Perhaps though I have said enough to suggest these two reflections,— first, that insofar as the world seems made for the mathematician's ease, he has made it so himself; secondly, that we are likely to need his genius to help us in making it over again. I leave him then in the hope that I have lifted a load from his shoulders. Let him not quarrel with his luck; for what is good in it isn't luck, and what is luck and accident isn't good.

JOURNALS OF FIRST PUBLICATION

I. Mind As An Observable Object, Journal of Philosophy, March, 1911.
II. Consciousness and Behavior, Journal of Philosophy, January, 1912.
III. On Mind As An Observable Object, Journal of Philosophy, April, 1912.
IV. The Pulse of Life, Journal of Philosophy, November, 1914.
V. On Sensibility, and
VI. Discussion of Sensation-Intensity, Journal of Philosophy, June, 1917.
VII. Pain and Dreams, Journal of Philosophy, to appear.
VIII. Man and Fellow-Man, Journal of Philosophy, March, 1913.
IX. Sensation and the Datum of Science, Philosophical Review, September, 1898.
X. Choice and Nature, Mind, January, 1902.
XI. On Mechanical Explanation, Philosophical Review, May, 1904.
XII. On Final Causes, Philosophical Review, May, 1902.
XIII. Kant's First Antinomy, Philosophical Review, July, 1909.
XIV. The Mathematician and His Luck, Mathematics Teacher, 1914-1915.

The author has permitted himself such changes in wording as taste might suggest and such suppression of paragraphs as made for brevity.

INDEX

absolutism, and instrumentalism, 138-143; and infinities, 147-149.
accident, 67, 261-263.
addition, not all composition is, 14-17, 61-63.
aesthetic, judgments, 192-198.
analogy argument, stated, iii, iv, 3; criticized, 3-5.
anodyne, as counter-stimulus, 123, 124.
Aquinas, on teleology, 241.
Aristotle, 54, 68, 82, 241, 263.
Augustin, *noli foras ire,* 143.
automatic, James on *a. sweetheart,* 7-10, 17.

behavior, mind *is,* 10.
behaviorism, relation to, vi, vii.
Bergson, on intensity of sensation, 116-120; criticized, 120-122.
Bichat, his definition of *life,* 38.
birth, not essential to life, 72-74.
Bohn, *conscience* and *psychisme,* 49, 50.
Bradley, on *possibility,* 166, 172.

Carpenter, rejects *vital principle,* 37.
cell-theory, in biology, 243-257.
chemistry, defined, 233-235.
choice, in science, 199-223, 288-293.
Church, and Copernican system, 210, 216, 217, 220.
classification, objects affected by, 203-209; of sciences, 229-238.
Clifford, on *inference* and *eject,* iii-vi. scientific construction, 157-159, 180-184.
Cossmann, *empirische Teleologie,* 46.

datum, immediate, 116, 118, 157-159; not immediate, 13, 14, 159-184; ideal, 280-282.
death, not essential to life, 72-74.
definition, ateleological and teleological, 57-60; pragmatic, 77.
Dewey, quoted, 137-138; questioned, 138-141.
dimensions, define sciences, 229-236.
dream-sensations, 128-133.

INDEX

Driesch, on *vitalism*, 248-254.

eject, defined, v, vi; criticized, 3-10, 47, 49, 167.
empirical idealism, viii, ix.
empiricism, radical, viii.

fact, immediate f. of consciousness, 22, 24, 118; of exact science, 199-207; unknowable, 43, 267; real ideal, 282.
Fechner, definition of sensation-intensity, 87-89, 113-119.
Fichte, 139, 140, 287.
field of consciousness, 22, 23.
freedom, defined, 61; implied in purpose, 60, 61, 112.

Galileo, 293, 294.
growth, and cell theory, 245, 246.

Hamiltonian principle, 214, 262.
Hankel, 211.
history, recoverable, 42, 43, 271-278; length of world-history, 273-278.
Hegel, on immediacy, 157, 183, 197, 219.

Helmholtz, sensation as *quale*, 169, 214n. .
higher, in biological scale, 79-82, 111, 112.
homology, and cell theory, 245.
Huxley, on Ptolemaic system, 210.

ideal, real as, 282; mechanical, 227-257.
idealism, empirical, viii, ix; Kantian, 280, 286.
immediate, fact of consciousness, 22, 24, 115, 161-176; no immediate datum, 13, 176-184.
immortality, 34, 35.
indifferentism, 192-198.
inference, Clifford on, iii-vi, 45.
infinity, actual and possible, 148-150.
instrumentalism, and absolutism, 138-143.
intensity, of stimulus defined, 85, 86; of sensation defined, 86-89, 101-106; Bergson quoted and criticized, 116-122.

James, pragmatic test of meaning, 6; criticism of, 6-9; on element of consciousness, 174-176, 182.

298

INDEX

Jennings, on reaction of paramecium, 89.

Kant, immediates, 182; *a priori*, 211; *Deduktion*, 218-220; fact, 267-282; two idealisms of, 280, 286.
Kepler, 209, 212, 216, 294.

Lagrangian, equations, 212, 262.
Laplace, on determinate system, 43, 44, 230-231, 211.
life, as *psyche*, 16; as vital principle, 16, 37-40; defined, by Bichat, 38, in terms of purpose, 57, 63, 64, 110; and mechanism, 55, 109-111; dormant, 37-40; lower and higher, 79-82, 111, 112.
Linnæus, on *true classification*, 208.
luck, made, 287-293.
Lucretius, 187.

Mach, on sensation, 162; on Copernican system, 210.
Maimon, datum as limit, 288.
mechanism, defined, 231; and life, 55, 109-111.
materialism, 56-60, 111,
mechanical ideal, defined, 227-238; opposed, 238-253; defended, 253-258.
mind, defined, 78-82, 111-113.
monadism, 56-60, 111, 257n. .
Miller, discussion of mind as object, 22-30.
Montague, materialism of mind-behavior theory, 54.
Montaigne, *le nom et la chose*, 204.
Morgan, on *regeneration*, 245.

Newton, 212-216, 244, 293, 294.
Nietzsche, 221.
noumenon, Kant on, 281-283.

objective, order, iv; teleology, 261-263.
Ormond, 34.

passive, thought, 35-50; sensibility, 92, 96; observation, 287, 289, 292.
Payne, on dormant life, 38-40.
Poincaré, on geomotry, 211n. .
polarity, in regeneration, 246.

299

INDEX

possibility, bare p. impossible, 148, 149, 166, 171.
post-Kantian, change from Kant, 218.
Prat, new monadology, 218n. .
probable behavior, *see* virtual.
progress, 220-223; 280-283.
psychophysics, 87-89, 101-106, 123, 124, 129, 130.
purpose, defined, 65-68; defining implements, 58; defining life, 57, 63, 64, 110.

quality, defined, 85; of stimulus, 86; of sensation, 93-95, 169.

radical empiricism, and empirical idealism, viii, ix.
real, as ideal, 280-283.
reduction of sciences defined, 237.
regeneration, in organisms, 246, 247.
Renouvier, new monadology, 257n. .
resource, of life defined, 112.
Royce, 141, 142.

Schleiden, cell theory of, 243.

Schwann, cell theory of, 243.
sciences, ateleological, defined, 58; classified, 229-233; teleological, defined, 58; method of, 64-69.
self-preservation, defined, 69-72; defining life, 63, 64, 69, 110.
sensation, not imemdiate, 163-176; defined, 82-85; -intensity, 85-89, 101-106, 122; -quality, 93-95; in dreams, 128-133.
sensualism, on English, 11-14.
social, reference of mind, 138-153.
soul, behavior and meaning of, 8-10; immortality of, 34, 35.
Spinoza, and materialism, 56n.; and freedom, 62n. .
subjective order, iv.

teleological, definition, 57; method objective, 261-263.
thing-in-itself, 165, 280-282.
thinker, the passive, 35-50.
tolerance, and science, 188-191.
true, choices, 207-223.

unknowable, 42, 43, 267, 280-282.

INDEX

virtual behavior, 91-93.
vitalism, 241-258.
vital principle, 16, 37-40.

Washburn, 35, 36.
Weber's law, 87, 102-106.

Whitman, on cell theory, 245-248.
will, in science, 215-223.
world, finite or infinite? 267-278.
Wundt, on sensation, 173, 176, 177.